PENGUIN MODERN CLASSICS

The Coming Age

C. SUBRAMANIA BHARATI (1882-1921) is considered the leading writer of the twentieth century in the Tamil language and is known to Tamils as the 'Mahakavi' ('Supreme Poet'). He was a nationalist who fought against British rule in India and a social reformer who advocated passionately for women's equality and the eradication of caste. His writings were proscribed by the British government and he lived in exile in the French Indian territory of Pondicherry for more than a decade. Bharati's innovative contributions to Tamil poetry and prose are considered to have sparked a Renaissance in twentieth-century Tamil literature.

MIRA T. SUNDARA RAJAN is a writer, a classical pianist, and a scholar and professor who holds a doctorate in law from Oxford University. A Canadian citizen by birth, she is fluent in English and French and has read both literatures extensively. She is the daughter of Bharati scholar S. Vijaya Bharati, and a great-granddaughter of Mahakavi Bharati.

C. SUBRAMANIA BHARATI

The Coming Age
COLLECTED ENGLISH WRITINGS

Edited by
Mira T. Sundara Rajan

PENGUIN BOOKS
An imprint of Penguin Random House

PENGUIN BOOKS

USA | Canada | UK | Ireland | Australia
New Zealand | India | South Africa | China

Penguin Books is part of the Penguin Random House group of companies
whose addresses can be found at global.penguinrandomhouse.com

Published by Penguin Random House India Pvt. Ltd
4th Floor, Capital Tower 1, MG Road,
Gurugram 122 002, Haryana, India

First published in Penguin Books by Penguin Random House India 2021

Copyright © Mira T. Sundara Rajan 2021

All rights reserved

10 9 8 7 6 5 4 3 2 1

The moral rights of the author have been asserted.

The views and opinions expressed in this book are the author's own and the
facts are as reported by him/her which have been verified to the extent possible,
and the publishers are not in any way liable for the same.

ISBN 9780143453406

Typeset in Adobe Garamond Pro by Manipal Technologies Limited, Manipal

www.penguin.co.in

For P.K. Sundara Rajan, who taught me English and literature, with love.

Contents

II. SOCIAL JUSTICE

III. PHILOSOPHICAL ESSAYS

VII. FROM BHARATI'S JOURNAL

Acknowledgements

This book owes a tremendous debt to S. Vijaya Bharati. A pioneering scholar of C. Subramania Bharati's works, Vijaya Bharati was in a unique position with respect to the poet. She was the first person to undertake the study of Bharati's works as a literary specialty, completing her doctoral thesis on him at Annamalai University in 1966, and she was also his granddaughter—daughter of Bharati's elder daughter, Thangammal Bharati.

Vijaya Bharati was therefore immersed in Bharati's work throughout her youth, even prior to her formal study of it. This fact is important because Bharati himself had initiated a family oral tradition for the preservation of his works, teaching them personally to his wife, Chellamma, and their two daughters. Vijaya Bharati was raised by both Thangammal and Chellamma, who lived with her daughter. From her mother and grandmother, she acquired a deep knowledge of Bharati's life and work; indeed, Chellamma had recounted Bharati's life story in *Bharatiyar Charithram*, which became Bharati's first published biography, composed by dictating the work to Thangammal.

From them, Vijaya Bharati also learned the poet's verses as Bharati, in keeping with the Indian tradition that unites poetry and music, originally sang them to his family. She was a highly gifted singer who preserved this oral tradition throughout her own life, intact.

It is difficult to describe the extent of Vijaya Bharati's immersion in Bharati's poetry. Her reading and writing as a scholar of Bharati was maintained intensively, continuously, and single-mindedly for a period of well over fifty years. It appeared that no word written by Bharati was unfamiliar to her, and she continued to reference his works from memory until her eightieth year.

Her learning, as well as her devotion, were extremely rare and precious qualities.

As Vijaya Bharati's only child, I have benefited immeasurably from the extraordinary treasure trove of knowledge about her grandfather that she amassed over these decades. Towards the end of her life, when she remained as active as ever, she became passionately interested in communicating Bharati's ideas to a wider audience beyond Tamil speakers, extending to India as a whole and, of course, the world. Perhaps like her grandfather, she was more interested in the future than in the past. She felt that the medium of English was a powerful means of communication that had not yet been adequately explored in relation to Bharati, and she set about doing so herself, in a series of new projects.

One of her cherished goals was to publish Bharati's original English writings in a new edition. She wanted to see these works appear in an authoritative and modern publication worthy of the poet's name. She asked me, her daughter, if I would edit the book and provide an introduction that would help readers from different backgrounds to appreciate Bharati's writings in context. To support this effort, she provided invaluable background information to many of the writings presented here, and she was intensively involved in advising on the preparation of this work in its earlier phases.

It is in fulfilment of her wishes as well as my own that I now present this collection to readers, hoping that they will enjoy reading, or re-reading, Bharati in his English incarnation.

My deepest gratitude is due to Premanka Goswami of Penguin Random House India, a true lover of Indian literature, and to his colleague Rea Mukherjee, without whose extraordinary support and encouragement this book could not have been published. Their work has been exemplary in all respects and to them, I offer my humble hope that the final product meets with their satisfaction.

All errors or omissions, of course, remain my own.

Brief Chronology of Life and Publications*

1882   Born in Ettayapuram on 11 December, Tirunelveli
        District (now Tamil Nadu, then Madras Province).
        His mother was Lakshmi Ammal and his father
        was Chinnasamy Iyer.

1887   Death of Bharati's mother, a loss that he felt deeply
        throughout his life.

1893   Title 'Bharati', meaning learned, wise, eloquent,
        conferred upon the young poet, at age eleven, by
        the scholars at the Ettayapuram Maharaja's court,
        where his father was employed. The name invokes
        Saraswati, Hindu goddess of learning, intellect,
        and the arts.

---

* This work is based on published and unpublished biographical research by
S. Vijaya Bharati, including the Annotated Biography available at https://
subramaniabharati.com (last visited 17 Jan. 2021).

1894–97   Studied at the Hindu College High School in
            Tirunelveli from Form III to Form V (Standard
            8 to 10).

1897   Married Chellamma, who was then seven years
            old; he was fourteen.

1898   Death of Bharati's father, Chinnawamy Iyer,
            following the failure of his cotton mill, established
            in Ettayapuram and put out of business by the
            British.

1898–1902   Invited to live with his aunt, Kuppammal, in
            Benares (Varanasi); studied at the Hindu College.

1902–04   Worked at the court of the Ettayapuram Maharaja.

1904   In August, Bharati became a Tamil teacher
            (*pundit*) at the Sethupati High School, Madurai,
            and worked there for three months. Birth of his
            first daughter, Thangammal, on 10 November.

1904–06   Joined *Swadesamitran,* in Chennai, as its sub-
            editor, under the editorship of its founder, G.
            Subramania Iyer, who had previously established
            The Hindu newspaper. *Swadesamitran* was among
            the first Tamil language newspapers, and the first
            founded by Indians.[1]

1905   Attended the Congress meeting held in Benares in
            December.

1905–06   Became the editor of *Chakravartini,* a Tamil
            Monthly in Chennai owned by P. Vaidyanatha
            Iyer.

1906   Became the editor of the *Bala Bharat,* an English
            weekly based in Chennai owned by Dr M.C.
            Nanjundarao. In December, attended the Congress
            meeting in Calcutta and, on his return journey,

met Sister Nivedita Devi, later the dedicatee of the first edition of his *National Poems*.

1906–08   Quit both *Swadesamitran* and *Chakravartini* to join *India* as editor, although, in order to protect the magazine from British interference, he was not named as such. The editor was officially M. Srinivasan.

1907   Three of his national poems published for the first time by V. Krishnasamy Iyer, the leader of the Moderate Party in the province of Madras.

1908   Published a collection of national songs, *Swadesa Githangal*. On 5 September, the publication of *India* was halted by the British government and its legal editor, M. Srinivasan, was arrested. Bharati moved to Pondicherry shortly therafter, and the publication of *India* was resumed from Pondicherry on 10 October. His second daughter was born; he named her Shakuntala, after the heroine of Kalidasa's Sanskrit epic.

1909   Published the second part of *Swadesa Githangal*, entitled *Janma Boomi*.

1909–10   Became the editor of the daily newspaper *Vijaya*, in Pondicherry.

1910   Established his own Tamil monthly, *Karma Yogi*, which he also edited. In March, *India* and *Vijaya* were proscribed in British India. Publication of these magazines ceased within the next month. *Kanavu*, his autobiographical poem, was published.

1911   *Kanavu* was proscribed, along with Bharati's short story entitled *Aril Oru Pangu*. A warrant was issued for all nationalists who lived in Pondicherry. There was also an announcement in British India of a bounty of one thousand rupees to be awarded to anyone who could help to capture the nationalists in Pondicherry.

1912   Part 1 of his epic poem, *Panchali Sabatham,* was published.

1913   Performed the *poonal* (sacred thread) ceremony for a 'Harijan' boy named Kanakalingam.

1914   *Maada Manivachagam,* a collection of poems, was published in Durban, South Africa by Saraswati Printing Press.

1917   First edition of *Kannan Pattu* was published by Parali Su. Nellaiyappar, a close friend of Bharati and Editor of *Lokopakari.*

1918   First edition of *Nattuppattu* was published by Parali Su. Nellaiyappar. In November, Bharati left Pondicherry and was arrested in Cuddalore, where he was imprisoned for twenty days. His friends secured his release from jail and he went immediately to the village of Kadayam in Tirunelveli district, the birthplace of his wife, Chellamma.

1919   In March, Bharati met Mahatma Gandhi in Chennai. In April and May, he traveled to Ettayapuram, where his relatives and friends wanted Bharati to seek the Maharaja's help. Although opposed to the idea, he nevertheless wrote two poems, called *Chittukkavigal,* and sent them to the Maharaja. In June, his elder daughter, Thangammal, who Bharati wanted to wed to a

'German prince', was married in the traditional way; Bharati officiated at the marriage himself.

1920   Bharati sent a 'circular' letter in English to his friends, dated 28 June, seeking financial support that would allow him to publish all of his writings. Nothing came of this effort. He returned to Chennai and resumed the sub-editorship of *Swadesamitran.*

1921   While visiting the Parthasarathy temple in Triplicane (Tiruvallikeni), Madras (Chennai), he was struck down by the temple elephant, which was unwell. The incident weakened him, and he developed a stomach ailment shortly afterwards. His death followed on 11 September.

Introduction

In 1908, C. Subramania Bharati, south India's foremost nationalist writer and the *Mahakavi* ('Supreme Poet') of the Tamils, went to live in exile in Pondicherry. By a strange irony, he gained, in abundance, a luxury that few writers have, and even fewer know how to use: time. He was to spend ten years in exile, in this relative backwater of French India, distanced from the heartland of the Freedom struggle in Madras province, and subject to various petty cruelties at the hands of the British operatives who crossed the border with the tacit consent of the French. Publication of Bharati's works had been proscribed in British India, where his main readership lay, and in Pondicherry, his professional activities as a journalist ground to a halt. Finally, in desperation, he returned to Madras, only to meet with death unexpectedly. He was not yet thirty-nine years old.

What he accomplished during that time in Pondicherry was almost miraculous. Struggling for subsistence, he nevertheless penned a number of pure literary masterpieces. The profound and philosophical *Kannan Pattu* ('Songs of Kannan') is a series of poems on Krishna as embodied in the various guises of lover, friend, parent, child, servant, and the other personalities of everyday life. The fantastic fable of the *Kuyil Pattu* ('Song of the Koel') describes the magical adventures of the koel bird and her lovers in a luxuriant mango grove.[1] *Panchali Sabadham* ('Panchali's Vow') was his feminist retelling of a notorious incident from the Mahabharata, when the vicious leader of the Kaurava princes attempts to insult Panchali, wife of the Pandava heroes, by disrobing her in public.[2] This last work is now considered a modern Tamil 'epic' in a tradition initiated more than 1500 years ago by Ilango Adigal in his *Silappadikaram* ('The Tale of the Anklet'), one of the classical 'five epics' of Tamil literature.

Bharati's poetry bursts open the confines of the classical Tamil language, surging with irresistible power and shimmering with the transparency that is the hallmark of all Bharati's writing—giving joyous birth to modern speech. His works deal comprehensively with human experience. They can be delightfully playful, filled with humor and fun. They develop thrilling narratives while also touching the deeper chords of love, tragedy, vice, redemption, and moral rebirth.

The personality that emerges is, to our knowledge, unique in world literature. Bharati is an exuberant optimist, his words sometimes tumbling over each other in their passionate eagerness of expression. He is an ecstatic lover of God and humanity. His compassionate outlook extends to every group and nation—even to the oppressive British rulers of his time. Love thine enemy, he wrote ('*pagaivanuk-arulvai*'), but this was no mere cliché; he lived by this command. He believed that Heaven is not in the afterlife, but here and now. He worked tirelessly towards the establishment of his goal, *Krita Yuga*, Heaven on Earth.

The modern world needs a writer like this. His literary gifts transport and transform us, affirming the wondrous possibilities of human experience. His world view is inspiring, but it is also something more than this: Bharati offers practical solutions to many of the defining problems of our era.

Among Tamil-speakers, Bharati's reputation is unrivaled. He is generally accepted as the leading figure in twentieth century Tamil literature, and he is also credited with generating a Renaissance in modern Tamil writing. Few writers in any language can lay claim to contributions of this magnitude.

It is therefore an enduring source of frustration for Bharati enthusiasts that the poet's work has not become better known worldwide. The reasons for this are, to some degree obvious. Bharati remains largely inaccessible to a broader audience behind the formidable linguistic barrier presented by his beloved native tongue, Tamil. A century after his death, quality translation, upon which writers outside the mainstream of Western literary currents inevitably depend, remains lacking.

Yet there are also broader considerations: the marginalization of literature in Indian languages more generally, and the gradual but steady erosion of south India's status in the world throughout the twentieth century. More than seven decades after Indian independence, not only Bharati, but also the incomparably rich Tamil culture that he embodied—which popular historian Michael Wood calls the world's last surviving classical civilisation[3]—continues to be largely inaccessible to the world.

Yet, in addition to his Tamil contributions, Bharati also wrote and published regularly in English, today's undisputed *lingua franca* of the globe. In contrast to his Tamil writings, these examples of the poet's original work are relatively little known. However, they are both valuable and exciting. The reasons for their relative neglect are complex; what is beyond doubt is the urgency of the need to rectify it. The dissemination of Bharati's English writings is a necessary part of making the poet's presence known as an important Indian writer, one who has a rightful place on the world stage. Accordingly, the purpose of this book is to present Bharati's English writings to readers in India and worldwide, in an authoritative, reliable, and modern publication. By doing so, this book also hopes to suggest the broader reality of a vibrant Indian literature in the national languages of India that developed, against extraordinary odds, during the period of colonial rule.

*

For a proper appreciation of Bharati's English writings, we must delve more deeply into the publication history of the poet's works as a whole. When Bharati died in 1921, most of his writing was still unpublished. The poet himself had wanted to assemble his collected works in an authoritative edition, but he was unable to complete this project before he died.

After his death, the task of publication was taken up by Bharati's wife, Chellamma. Chellamma made heroic efforts towards this goal, in the process revealing herself to be, as Bharati had indeed anointed her, the 'heroine' of her husband's poetry (*kavithai thalaivi*). However, as a woman and a widow in 1920s India, Chellamma faced virtually insurmountable obstacles. The pressures of life eventually overcame her and she was compelled, very much against her will, to abandon publication. She sold the copyright in Bharati's works, for a negligible sum, to a group of male relatives, headed by Bharati's half-brother, Viswanatha Iyer.

Viswanatha Iyer published many of Bharati's works. However, he eventually sold the copyright to the Madras government,[4] which published most of Bharati's Tamil writings, both poetry and prose, but left a few works unpublished. The latter included Bharati's writings in English. The editorial supervision of the government's publishing project was undertaken by a specially appointed committee, but the committee's work was challenging and sometimes controversial.

The government, like those who had previously attempted publication, abandoned this project before it was complete. It then took a truly unprecedented step: it 'gave' the copyright in Bharati's work to the people of India as a gift. This meant that any Indian citizen would have the right to publish Bharati's works. It is only fitting to note that it had been Chellamma's own intention to bequeath Bharati's copyright to the public after her death.[5] In this sense, the story seemed to have reached a somewhat satisfactory conclusion.

But Chellamma's true goal, faithful publication of the poet's original work, had yet to be fully realized. Instead, a rush of Bharati publication after Indian independence served a burgeoning mass-market industry in south India, with little concern for preserving the integrity of the poet's works. This continued to be the case into the twenty-first century, when the first edition of Bharati's poetry that can lay claim to being truly authoritative, in the sense that Bharati and Chellamma might have understood this term, was finally published by the poet's own granddaughter, eminent Bharati scholar S. Vijaya Bharati.[6] Vijaya Bharati chose to publish her new edition independently, a feat of no small significance,[7] and a fascinating turn of events in the continuing life of Bharati's poems more than one hundred years after the poet's death.

It was Viswanatha Iyer who first edited and (re-)published much of Bharati's original writing in English, which appeared in 1937 as part of the Bharati Prachuralayam edition.[8] This was done as an afterthought to the overall project of publishing Bharati's Tamil works. As the centenary of Bharati's birth approached in 1982, various honors were conferred on the poet's memory. At this time, his English works were brought out in a new collection, *Agni and Other Poems*.[9]

What were these English writings, exactly, by the Tamil *Mahakavi*? The writing that Bharati did in English is rather different from his Tamil works. Bearing in mind that Bharati's primary professional activity was journalism, much of his work in English takes the form of short essays and articles that were suitable for magazine and newspaper publication. The magazines in which he published included *Arya, Commonweal,* and *New India,* and they were run by fellow nationalists such as Annie Besant and Sri Aurobindo Ghose.

Within this framework, however, Bharati's English essays touch upon an astonishing variety of themes. They deal with contemporary political issues, as well as Indian history and culture, social issues, and the Tamil language. They reveal a side of the poet that may be unfamiliar even to his readers in Tamil. The Subramania Bharati of the English writings is cosmopolitan and well-informed, widely knowledgeable of world affairs and passionately opinionated about them. His English essays demonstrate the extraordinary breadth of his reading in at least four languages—Tamil, English, French, and Sanskrit—and his uncanny ability to move smoothly between different cultures and eras. He compares ancient *Vedic* thought with contemporary German philosophy, examines India's sacrifices in the first World War, explores cosmic science and folk religion, and contrasts Indian cultural renewal with the disintegration of European culture. Perhaps as a result of his sojourn in francophone Pondicherry, he was profoundly influenced by French humanist thinkers. He seems to sense the impending evils of European Nazism, while his ideals of caste, gender, and religious equality remain, in some respects, even ahead of *our* time.

In many of these preoccupations, Bharati takes his place alongside the great European and American writers and humanists of his era. He is engaged in a lively dialogue with E.M. Forster and Virginia Woolf, reflects a shared spirituality with Walt Whitman and Ralph Waldo Emerson, exudes the refinement of Rainer Maria Rilke and T.S. Eliot in his own poetic experiments, and argues (explicitly in the essay 'The Siddha and the Superman') with Friedrich Nietzsche.

Although cultural criticism traditionally separates East and West, these writers and thinkers lived at a shared moment in human history and saw the world from their different perspectives (literally) around the globe. At the turn of the twentieth century, the common destiny of humanity as citizens of the Earth, increasingly obvious today, was becoming apparent. The very research of the Orientalists, beginning with the gigantic contributions of the German scholar Max Muller, laid bare the ancient connections between Western and Eastern culture, symbolized by the shared linguistic heritage of the classical Sanskrit language. It was no accident that Eliot's 'Waste Land', the emblematic Western poem of that era, reflects, among other things, its author's meditations on Indian philosophy.

The publication of these English essays must have brought Bharati some means of livelihood, but his aims were far more ambitious. Bharati's approach to the national struggle was, fundamentally, that of a *writer*. One of his chief objectives when writing in English was, therefore, to write for a British audience—to show the British rulers just who these governed Indians were and how they felt about British rule, to expose the unfounded and utterly misguided nature of British claims to cultural superiority.

Accordingly, Bharati's writing in English is a celebration of Indian excellence, but it is also a carefully reasoned campaign of argument against the so-called justifications of British rule. It is critical, in the best sense of the word, of all that it touches, evaluating the claims and counterclaims of Indians and British in the most objective terms. The importance of this exercise can hardly be overstated. Bharati was living in an era when pure violence, the currency of the early conquest of India, had been subsumed by a greater moral discourse in which British administrators sought to justify their presence in India to an increasingly skeptical intelligentsia and public. Crucially, they were under siege, not only in India, but also at home— in Britain. It was an argument that the British rulers of India could not win.

*

A number of the essays in this collection deal with incidents that were significant to the national struggle. Among the most important of these is the long essay 'The Political Evolution in the Madras Presidency'. The origins of this essay lie in a sudden act of violence—the murder of district collector Ashe by a south Indian activist, Vanchi Iyer, who committed suicide after his crime. This incident terrorized the British administration in south India, triggering an intense escalation of repression against the nationalist community. The attack, writes Bharati, created 'a situation very like hell in

Pondicherry'. He, like other nationalists, was suspected of complicity in the murder.

Discussing both the background to this incident and its consequences, Bharati's essay provides an incisive and disturbing overview of the freedom struggle in south India up to that point. It tells a story that, as far as we are aware, has never been told with such clarity before or since. Describing the confrontation between British and Indians in stark terms, he shows how the Ashe murder stirred 'instinctive and atavistic racial fears and animosities' in the ruling population, propelling the British down a path of unreasoned brutality that Indians could never forget.

In this essay, Bharati's fury finds an eloquent voice. Who knew that he could be so sarcastic? Writers on British history still talk, occasionally, of the 'beneficial' effects of British rule for India. Bharati writes that the British 'fiat' was 'Repress! Imprison, deport, hang!' And he comments:

> 'How wise it would have been on the part of the British authorities at that period if they had adopted a policy of clear-sightedness, of justice, and of humanity! Had they but punished the actual perpetrators of crime and then left things alone, the subsequent history of India would have run on lines much more favourable to the British. But Fate had ordained otherwise.'

On a more personal note, Bharati wrote directly to Ramsay MacDonald, then leader of the (opposition) British Labour Party in England, to protest the operation of censorship against him in south India, including the proscription of the Pondicherry-based journals in which he had been publishing.

Once again, Bharati describes the aftermath of the Ashe murder case, with which the government had wrongfully linked him. He laments, 'I wish I had sufficient power of language to depict the whole absurdity and injustice of the thing.' Imagine Bharati, the Mahakavi, at a loss for words. He continues, 'I have heard and read about many countries and I may record my sincere conviction that nowhere in the world is the sacredness of individual liberty more cynically ignored than in Madras and certain other Provinces of India.'

Such was the character of British rule in south India—and such was the fate of the freedom-fighters, prisoners in their own country, starved and silenced. India and the world should remember these happenings, because freedom today, in a very real sense, has only been made possible by the sacrifices of these people and others like them. What Bharati describes is no mere idea of sacrifice; it is a provocative, first-hand narration of life as he saw and lived it, a life in which sacrifice was inevitable for those who sought freedom. Ever the journalist, Bharati offers a painstaking and probing reportage of the events that he saw unfolding around him—even as he himself was caught in the spinning of the cyclone.

Bharati, the master craftsman, is also keenly present in these works. With the exception of the historical articles noted above, most of the essays are brief pieces—a few hundreds of words, what the French might call *esquisses,* mere sketches. But what he can accomplish in those fleeting moments is quite startling. A short essay like 'Rasa' conveys the essence of Indian culture, in all its antiquity, in all its aspiration. An entire philosophy of life is laid bare and delivered up, almost as a personal exhortation to the reader, in the plainest of concluding words: 'The trembling coward is wasting the same material he could be using to make himself a hero.' 'The Dawn' anatomizes the phenomenon of Renaissance, a historical movement experienced by different peoples at different times, through an exploration of the 'deathless imagery of the seer Viswamitra', who writes of the coming of dawn in the Rig Veda. For Bharati, Renaissance is an all-encompassing experience, and he is able to convey its many dimensions—historical, intellectual, emotional, national, and personal—in a few simple words. His style is direct and unpretentious, and his words come straight from the heart. These essays are gems.

At times, Bharati's engagement with English becomes intensely personal. In 'Journal of Thoughts', he addresses some of his most fundamental preoccupations, death and immortality, mental discipline, and the development of the self. It is interesting, and a bit mystifying, that he chose to deal with these ideas in English. But this is perhaps the value of fluency in multiple tongues: languages represent different ways of thinking, and the English language provided Bharati with a novel means of exploring his deepest concerns.

Bharati's writing shows that he never thought of himself in narrowly nationalistic terms. And, indeed, his progressive social ideals, and his determination to put them into practice—sometimes radically, as when he inducted his 'Harijan' disciple Kanagalingam into the Brahmin tradition with a *poonal* (sacred thread) ceremony—thoroughly antagonized parts of his own society. At times, he was compelled to live as an outcaste. The essays in this collection celebrate the equality of all human beings, women with men, so-called outcastes with Brahmins, Indians with British. Inevitably, he writes of the intense joy of freedom from oppression, as when he calls to the women enjoying the traditional folk dance known as the *kummi* to dance in celebration: 'We sing the joys of freedom; / In gladness we sing.' At a time when gender and caste equality were overwhelmingly important issues for Indians, it can still be said that no Indian reformer was more outspoken than Bharati. His mind, perhaps as a result of his visionary experiences as a poet, was 'incandescent', to expand upon Virginia Woolf's use of the expression—absolutely free of prejudice of any kind.[10]

He was engaged with the world at large; he belonged to it, and he wanted to be situated alongside the leading thinkers of his time, whether European or American. English was the language of empire; for better or for worse, it was the language of global currency. But it was also the embodiment of Englishness, whatever that meant. For Bharati, it was perhaps a way of writing without bearing the ponderous weight of Tamil heritage upon his shoulders—a way of expressing his thoughts that was plainer and more raw, a look at his own mind in its nakedness.

Some of the most remarkable pieces in this collection attempt something else altogether: the translation of great Tamil writing and ideas into English. Written at the height of empire, these essays and translations seem to be aimed directly at a *post-colonial* audience, speaking mind to equal mind with English-speaking readers who want to experience the beauty of Tamil literature and culture for themselves. They range from his fascinating discussion of the 'occult' elements in the Tamil language, exploring the hidden significance of everyday Tamil speech, to his peerless translations of Tamil devotional poets. 'Love-Mad' might easily dissolve the reader in tears, as Nammalwar, Tamil poet-saint of the eighth century, describes a girl's enraptured obsession with the ineffable Lord Krishna. Andal's 'Wedding-Day' is rendered with thrilling joy.[11]

In these translations, Bharati's English reaches a new level of directness and simplicity. It is absolutely stripped-down and bare, devoid of even the smallest superfluous gesture. It reflects the same sensibility that defines his Tamil writing—clarity, perfect clarity, sublime clarity. Paradoxically, the Writer seems to disappear, and we are left face-to-face with ultimate reality. No one but Bharati could have crafted translations like these. They are based on a profound reading of Tamil poetry and are typical of Bharati's English style at its best.

Bharati also tried his hand at translating his own poems, but the decision to include these translations in the present book was not a straightforward one.[12] In contrast to his prose writings, Bharati's poetic translations of his own work can make for challenging reading. While the poet maintains his simple and direct style in English, the poems are infused with Indian philosophical terms, either in the original Sanskrit or in English translation, and immersed in Indian symbolism and mythology. Bharati repeatedly invokes the 'feet' of the Divine Being, and non-Indian readers must come to understand the symbolic significance of those 'Lotus Feet', which permeates Indian culture. God is most often invoked as the Feminine Principle of Parashakti, a notable contrast with Judeo-Christian culture (which still has its undivine yet beloved Mother, Mary). All of this reflects deep characteristics of Indian culture that may be unfamiliar, awkward, or even jarring to Western readers. Of course, the imagery can also be interesting, novel, and inspiring. It all depends on how the reader responds—whether *you* are able to see through these details to the inner reality of the poem, and of the poet's heart.

That essential effort is made more complicated by the fact that the poetic craft employed in these translations can feel rudimentary—in contrast to Bharati's Tamil poetry. The language in some of these efforts comes across as dated; one fears the invocation of stereotypes of Indian culture that Western critics have long and improperly imposed on Indian literature. These stereotypes, aided by inadequate translation, are largely behind Rabindranath Tagore's fall from grace among Western literati, a fate from which even the award of the Nobel Prize has not been able to save him.[13] As Amartya Sen observes:

> Given the vast range of his creative achievements, perhaps the most astonishing aspect of the image of Tagore in the West is its narrowness; he is recurrently viewed as 'the great mystic from the East,' an image with a putative message for the West, which some would welcome, others dislike, and still others find deeply boring. To a great extent this Tagore was the West's own creation, part of its tradition of message-seeking from the East, particularly from India, which – as Hegel put it – had 'existed for millennia in the imagination of the Europeans'.[14]

However, apart from their shared belief in fundamental human values, Bharati and Tagore could not have been more different as poets and as men.

In the case of Bharati's translations, was the cultural gap, which is also reflected in the structural differences between Tamil and English, simply too large to bridge? 'Indeed,' Bharati writes, 'the genius of the Tamil tongue hardly permits of an effective rendering, so utterly divergent is it from that of the English language.' Is Bharati's poetry fundamentally untranslatable? If so, can the same be said about Tamil poetry in general?

As the editor of Bharati's English, I do not believe this to be the case. For example, as noted above, Bharati's own translations of other Tamil poets in this book are particularly fine. However, the evidence on Bharati translations is not really on my side. Many attempts at translating Bharati's poems into English have been made, but almost all of them are, to put it plainly, failures.[15] Still, there are a handful of exceptions, suggesting that successful English translation of his poetry is not impossible. It is encouraging that south Indian culture is becoming better known around the world—a process that has begun with the spread of the usual stereotypes, but that will hopefully extend to the dissemination of the deeper qualities inherent in this uniquely rich and ancient culture—and the growing familiarity of readers with its imagery and symbolism will help.

Moreover, Bharati not only deserves but needs to be translated by a writer of stature in English; expertise in Tamil is a necessary condition for this undertaking, but it is far from sufficient. A unique person or team of authors is needed to bridge the gap between Bharati's world, as expressed in his Tamil, and the distant world of English poetry and culture. Yet Bharati would certainly have felt that it is a journey worth making; this, at least, is demonstrated by his own efforts at translation. The examples in this book serve as interesting and helpful introductions to his work, and they also reveal his conception of translation—knowledge of value to his future translators.

In the present group of translations, we can find excerpts from some of Bharati's most significant works—*Kannan Pattu,* and a handful of translations of his individual masterpieces in Tamil. However, not one of these works is translated in its entirety. Many of these translations have the look of a rough draft, a *brouillon,* that Bharati never had the time to polish into a more finished form. One wonders whether the visionary poet could have imagined how much it would matter to future generations to be able to read some of his work in English.

The English written by Bharati reflects his education and his times. In editing, my overriding purpose has been to preserve the character and authenticity of Bharati's own words, presenting them in a modern format that will make them accessible to today's readers. Much has changed over the last century, even as far as the English language is concerned. Today, Indian writers of English have established a distinguished tradition of writing in this language, and have gone on to claim many of the world's most prestigious literary prizes in competition with Anglophone and international writers from around the world. Gone are the days when Yeats could assert with impunity, 'Tagore does not know English, no Indian knows English.'[16]

Moreover, the spirit of the times has changed dramatically. Today, at least, it should be understood—notwithstanding the exceptional successes of Indian writers writing in English—that non-Anglophone writers need be under no special obligation to strive to write English like their Anglophone peers. To judge them by standards such as these makes little sense. Their goals are fundamentally different: to bring the culture and imagination of precisely that non-Anglophone reality within touching distance of English readers. Their language must be appropriate for this purpose. Indeed, a century after Bharati's death, it is questionable whether we can even speak of the English language in quite the monolithic terms that Yeats seems to understand it. The language, always flexible and dynamic in reflection of the global ambitions of its progenitors, has now been transformed by the influence of those originally under its influence. In the process, its capacity to communicate and to bring communities together has actually grown, without in any way compromising the beauty and originality of the language of Shakespeare and of the 'English poets'.[17]

And so, we come full circle. Bharati, the Tamil Mahakavi, in the brief time available to him, became an English writer, and his own most reliable translator. These achievements are presented in this book. We hope that they will help him to take his place among the leading lights of twentieth-century Indian literature—and as one of the *phares,* in Baudelaire's terms, of humanity, for all times and all places.

Mira T. Sundara Rajan
San Francisco, California
30 July 2020

I

The National Movement

1

The Political Evolution in the Madras Presidency

The province of Madras is today regarded as the chief stronghold of Indian nationalism. But this has not always been so. About ten years ago, it was usual among the few Madrasi nationalists to lay much stress on the epithet 'benighted' as applied to Madras in view of the stolid resistance offered by Madras moderatism to all ingress of the new nationalist doctrines. Moderate Madras, at that period, had the good luck of being led by men like my friend, the late Mr V. Krishnaswamy Iyer, who died a government Executive Councillor. Mr Iyer's genuine and passionate support of the government against the attack of seditious and revolutionary forces did not make him lose the confidence of a large number of his own countrymen as a sincere and true-souled lover of India, the ancient Motherland. Mr V. Krishnaswamy Iyer, who was then the distinguished leader of the Madras Bar, had the good fortune, rare and almost inexplicable, of being the favourite and trusted counsellor of the Government and, at the same time, an accredited leader of a popular party—popular at that time, though not now. Mr V. Krishnaswamy

Iyer was a convinced Moderate, an honest believer in the virtues of conciliation and gradual progress under the British aegis. Any other alternative in the political destiny had an alarming prospect for him. His transparent sincerity won for him the admiration of friend and foe alike. He had a commanding mien; he was one of the greatest orators and most successful advocates of his time; he had a reputation for his deep learning in Sanskrit culture and philosophy; he made an immense fortune at the Bar and spent his money lavishly like a prince on all kinds of charitable objects. He had a big frame and stentorian voice—a winning personality on the whole, who, as has been remarked by some of his European admirers, would have risen to the highest stations of life in any country and in any age. All these combined to render Mr V. Krishnaswamy Iyer a formidable and dreaded opponent of the new party—or the 'Extremist Party', as he familiarly called it.

Thus, in the city of Madras and other important towns of the Presidency, the new nationalist movement was held in check by the moderate forces when Bengal and the Maharashtra were plunging headlong into it. It was only among the Tamil-reading middle classes, merchants, landlords, elementary school teachers, petty traders, lawyers' clerks, etc., as well as a large section of the Tamil-reading ladies, that the new political movement gained much support and adhesion, owing, chiefly, to the labours of the Tamil journals, *Swadesamitran* and *India.* The former, which is still the leading Tamil daily of the Presidency, was, at that time, edited by the veteran journalist, G. Subrahmania Iyer. It preached the new gospel, of course, and was almost about to be prosecuted on that score. But it could not cut itself altogether away from its old moderate moorings. And, consequently, it was not looked upon by the younger generation as quite representative of the visions and aspirations of India. That role was taken up by the other weekly journal *India,* which openly advocated complete liberty to be achieved by constitutional methods, of course, but methods quite different from the mendicancy of the Congress.

The latter journal is since deceased. After being prosecuted in Madras and having its editor sent to prison for five years, the journal was taken to Pondicherry by its conductors. And, there, in spite of my protests, its conductors permitted very 'strong' things to appear in the journal; and so, it was proscribed by the British government. Although its place of publication was the solitary French Indian town, most of its subscribers lived in British India. The British government's proscription, therefore, meant death for the paper.

Meanwhile, when the first bomb ever used by Indian terrorists was thrown, by sheer mistake, on a European lady, Mrs Kennedy by name, it made Anglo-India almost desperate with rage. And, indeed, what a pity it was! What a commentary on the re-awakened sense of Rajput chivalry in the heart of New India! What a woeful mistake! A bomb thrown at a woman for freeing India! And yet, the deepest cult of the Indian spiritual consciousness is one that calls upon us to revere every woman of whatever caste, colour, or country she might be, as a direct manifestation—or, to put it more correctly, the most direct manifestation—of the Divine Mother of the Universe, known to Hindu philosophy as 'Adi Shakti', the primordial force, the Divine Feminine. And India, with her age-long sense of the aesthetics of life, sometimes miscalled superstition, at once declared: 'Now, this is an inauspicious beginning. This movement will not thrive in my land. And some of the revolutionaries, too—ay, even the very leader of the first batch of Bengali terrorists, Mr Barindra Kumar Ghose, brother of the famous Aurobindo Ghose, expressed his intense regret at that time that the first bomb should have struck down a woman. He and his brother-workers, being of the emotional type themselves, could not but feel that mistake as a bad omen.

By the way, it is interesting to note that this same Barindra Kumar Ghose is now living in Calcutta, a free citizen, after serving a long term of imprisonment in the Andamans, in connection with the said inauspicious bomb. Since his release from the Andamans, his ideas seem to have developed into the very reverse of what they formerly were. Of his present doctrines and hopes, he sometimes writes to the chief Moderate journal of Calcutta, the *Bengali*. It would appear that he is hardly a nationalist nowadays. A patriot he certainly continues to be, but not a 'nationalist' in the modern European sense of the term. He has given up the bomb cult, and entirely believes, with his illustrious brother, in a coming spiritual change in the nation's mind whereby India will be rendered mighty in every department of human life, political or other, by methods and processes non-political, non-military, non-aggressive, and purely spiritual and, at the same time, abrupt, sudden, and dramatic. What exactly those methods and processes were and how they were going to find application on a national scale have not yet been made clear to the public by either of the brothers. But, I fancy, the above is quite sufficient to indicate that the Bengali terrorist movement which suddenly raised its head in 1908 and caused many dangerous and unfortunate upheavals and splits in the political life of India has now become as much a matter of ancient history as the continent called Atlantis.

The few later bombs of the Bengali terrorists and the fewer bombs handled by their Mahratta and other imitators, being mostly tentative and hypothetical bombs, did not burst at all in many cases. And even when they did burst, they were often not responsible for so much as a scratch on the victim's body. The bazaar people laughed as they heard of these bombs. But to the police or a considerable section of it, especially among the C.I.D. men,[1] this offered too tempting an opportunity for misrepresentations of a profitable character. They began to act in a manner which, while it proved many things about the policemen themselves, also proved that the Britishers in India were so far from identifying with the Indian people that they could most easily be led to believe in any of the most impossible misrepresentations made against the latter by hireling informers and worse folk. For the moment, the minds of the British rulers in India were possessed by a strange and hypnotic fear expressed in the vague terms 'the incomprehensible East'. From fear to severity is hardly a step. Soon, the government started a policy of repression and terror in almost every province in India, they penalized the whole country for the too-elaborately confessed sins of Barindra Kumar and his handful of Russianized fellow-conspirators in Bengal. Nationalist speakers and nationalist journals were prosecuted and subjected to severe punishment everywhere, even in benighted Madras. Of course, if the British officials in India felt that there was absolutely no chance of their getting unified with the Indian people; if, voluntarily or otherwise, they felt that the gulf of misunderstanding between the two races was unbridgeable; and if, in addition to this, they apprehended at any time that these Indians, constituting a tremendous majority of 320 million human beings, were in serious danger of being infected by the seditious cult of bomb-throwing—then, indeed, we can see that there would be hardly any chance of sound and conciliatory statesmanship being displayed by these officials. And the result was that they resolved upon the grim and fateful policy of ruthless repression. The strong ties of good will that had grown between the Indian and British communities during generations of considerate policy suddenly snapped to pieces. To India that stood expectant of gracious reforms and concessions at the hands of the British, the Anglo-Indian representatives of the British nation offered the bitter rod of punishment, merely because a few youths of Bengal played at bomb-throwing. How wise it would have been on the part of the British authorities at that period if they had adopted a policy of clear-sightedness, of justice, and of humanity! Had they but punished the actual perpetrators of crime and then left things alone, the subsequent history of India would have run on lines much more favourable to the British. But Fate had ordained otherwise. The officials of the Madras Presidency, especially, with whom we are most concerned here, began to feel furiously and act precipitately. To think that these Indians—whether they be Madrasis or Bengalis does not make a difference—that these men should renounce their usual role of tax-paying and low-*salaam*ing and presume to rebel! And, as the average official of the Madras Presidency began to query himself: 'What is happening to these "mild Hindus"? Where are their traditional smile, *salaam,* and servility? What is this new demon which seems to have taken possession of them? Why have they suddenly become so insolent, so impudent? Bombs for us, indeed, and no garlands this time. We will teach these monkeys a lesson which they will keep fresh in their memory for the next two centuries!' And forth goes the fiat: Repress! Imprison, deport, hang! The immediate result, of course, was what alone could be expected—the people were dumbfounded by terror. Peace, of course, was established; peace of a kind.

But concord had gone. All sorts of instinctive and atavistic racial fears and animosities were brought to the surface. The petty and miserable attempts at a schoolboys' rebellion were crushed out utterly. But this insignificant result was reached at a tremendous cost!

In the Madras Presidency, as in other Provinces, the nationalist speakers and the national press were very roughly dealt with. Mr G. Subrahmania Iyer, the great publicist, who then was a much ailing man, far advanced in years, was arrested on a charge of having published seditious articles in his newspaper the *Swadesamitran,* mentioned above. But he was released within a short period, after being put to the humiliation of having to sign an apology plus an undertaking. And this, too, became possible only by the strong recommendations of Mr V. Krishnaswamy Iyer, the Moderate leader, who promptly intervened on behalf of his great and afflicted rival, thus adding another proof to the great nobility of his character. The other journal, the Tamil weekly *India,* was forced to take refuge in Pondicherry, the capital of French India. Several other well-known patriots were also sentenced to harsh and prolonged terms of imprisonment of both kinds. The most prominent among these was the affair of the King vs. V.O. Chidambaram Pillai. He is a Tamil patriot whom Mr Pinhey, District Sessions Court Judge of Tinnevelly, sentenced to transportation for life twice, so to say—or, as the people accustomed to the Indian transmigration theory jokingly said, 'for two lives'— consecutively, the judge was kind enough to emphasize.[2] This barbarous and shockingly meaningless double-life punishment, dealt on two scores, of course, was considerably modified by the High Court of Madras, who eventually reduced it to five years' imprisonment, rigorous.[3]

Added to this was the fright produced in the public mind of the Presidency by the ruthlessly repressive policy and measures adopted by the governments of the other provinces. All this resulted, or tended to result, in the level-headed people of Madras dropping the new nationalistic creed as a piece of hot coal touched unwittingly. They soon contrived to forget all about *swadeshi* (nationalism) and *swaraj* (self-rule). Even the national cry of 'Bande Mataram' which, during the years 1907 and 1908, filled the sky everywhere and on all occasions, had become very rare indeed even by the end of the year 1908. It gradually came to be all but forgotten by the populace, as people realized that the authorities, or at least many of them, did not relish its use.

The people, on the one hand, terrified by the sudden phenomenon of reckless repression and, on the other, coaxed by the sweet blandishments of prosperous moderatism as signally exemplified as well as sonorously expounded by leaders like Mr V. Krishnaswami Iyer, soon turned pronouncedly moderate in their political views, aspirations, and activities, and the loyalist flag floated very high in the air.

The 'Ashe Murder' Case

It was at this favourable juncture of affairs that an unfortunate 'incident' (or should I say 'accident'—for the like of it never once recurred in our province) occurred. In the southernmost district of India, at the Maniachi Railway Station, Mr Ashe, Collector of Tinnevelly, was shot dead by an Indian, Vanchi Iyer. Now, this was a tragedy which, quite apart from its terrible political consequences, also had pathetic traits from the social and human points of view. Collector Mr Ashe of Tinnevelly, who was travelling with none but his wife in his company, was taking a pleasure trip or a health trip to Kodaikanal, a famous sanatorium situated in the adjacent district of Madura[i]. Again—an outrage to the Hindu religion; for the murdered man had his wife by his side. They were a young and, to all appearance, a loving couple. They were having a pleasure trip in each other's company. A scene like that would very profoundly appeal to the heart of the devout Hindu.

Lord Siva, the supreme God of good, is reported by the Hindu seers as being half Himself and half His other half, His consort. Siva is God; his consort in Hindu theology signifies his active energy literally known as Para-Shakti, or Supreme Energy, in the Hindu scriptures. 'Man and wife, when found together, form objects of worship to every Hindu, because they most really represent the state of Heaven.' And Hinduism is quite right. For, let a man and a woman but sincerely love each other and you will find them a very edifying and solemn spectacle while in each other's company. They will irradiate the whole atmosphere with love. Now, let us turn from the pathetic to the tragic in the story. A few minutes after killing the collector, Vanchi Iyer, after successfully intimidating those who attempted to arrest him, committed suicide by shooting himself dead. To the credit of the Madras Presidency, [it must be] state[d] immediately that a second incident of this character has not occurred since then. The terrorist movement in the Madras Presidency was stillborn. But the suicide of Vanchi Iyer had an unfortunate effect on the public life of this province. It left the police without a clue as to the actual accomplices of Vanchi Iyer. The officials, of course, wanted a sacrifice to be started in the regular Eastern fashion—and the police, the Indian police, made the sacrifice very elaborate indeed considering the number of victims, the extent of the field of operations, the amount of money spent, and so on, right through the whole analogy of the Hindu *yagna*. Arrested certain people must be; that is the initial process in this affair. But the police did not quite know whom to arrest. So they said to themselves something to the following effect: Let us arrest the whole population of this Tinnevelly district, and then the actual accomplices, prompters, and helpers, and it is certain there are lots and lots of them, are bound to get into their midst unerringly. But there was an unexpected trouble which upset the police argument completely. And that is, they could not arrest the population of an entire district. Bah! Were they to be foiled by such a trifle as that? They threw logic into the sea and determined, as a measure wherein justice and expediency are sweetly combined, to arrest as many people in the district as possible. But, eventually, lots of the people got themselves released by various appliances and the police were able to frame actual charges against a score or so of people. Some among them were convicted by the courts and the others let off. But the most curious part of the story is that none among these could be proved to have been guilty of actual abetment in the murder of Mr Ashe. On that charge, the High Court declared every one of them 'not guilty'. But what they called a side story developed, and some of those men were found guilty of a general conspiracy for the overthrow of the British government.

And, as a sequel to this, there followed an episode which it would be very advantageous to the good fame of the British administration in the province to forget once and for all. But, unfortunately, I hardly think this will be possible. The spirit of history is exacting.

Anyway, I shall content myself here with narrating the bare outlines of this episode and that, as succinctly as possible. The police subsequently held a new theory as regards their inability to find out the real abettors of Vanchi Iyer, and, of course, there were bound to be lots and lots of them somewhere—for the very apt reason that they were not in British India at all. No! They were in the little lovely town on the Coromandel Coast, Pondicherry, capital of French India. The authorities, who were under the intoxicating influence of a vague and nameless fear, easily fell into the net laid out for them by the police. They implicitly believed in the police stories and acted in accordance with the police advice. An understanding was entered into with the French government in Paris, whereby the British government in India were permitted to maintain a police force counting about two hundred at Pondicherry for an indefinite period—say, until, by some means or other, the said political refugees might be driven out of Pondicherry into British India. The British Indian police force, stationed at Pondicherry and calling its lodge a 'mahal' (palace), behaved like an army of occupation and was allowed to do so by the Pondicherry administration for various reasons. Firstly, of course, the *Entente Cordiale* was in full swing—we are speaking of the period between 1904 and 1914.[4] The war had not yet started. But it was in the atmosphere in various signs. So even in Europe, the Parisian ministers were so very desirous of winning the good graces of the British ministers that they were prepared to do anything to please the latter. This was openly spoken of in the schools and the markets, as well as the offices and societies, of Pondicherry. They even said that, in order to facilitate the falling of the British Indian refugees into the hands of the British Indian government, as well as to solve certain old difficulties regarding customs, etc., France intended to cede away Pondicherry to Britain in return for some big territory elsewhere. This sort of territorial adjustment had so many administrative and other conveniences about it that it would certainly have been effected but for the sentimental objection of France to giving away the town held by Dupleix as his capital.[5] The military-administrative glories of the French genius were displayed in the history of Pondicherry as certainly as in the history of Paris—the difference being merely one of quantity not of quality. So, the cession which—at one time, at any rate—came very near to realization and made the 'Mahe' policemen revel with anticipated joy, did not come about in the end because the sentiment for Dupleix and so on proved too strong.[6]

Part II

This police force cost the government of Madras something like one *lakh* of rupees each year.[7] The authorities were evidently made to believe that the money was well spent, as it was used for checking the dangerous seditious activities of the political suspects in Pondicherry. The police were sending daily reports— imagine about two hundred men solely engaged in collecting information and supplying daily reports about the exiles in Pondicherry who, after all, did not number more than five or six. You may be sure that, under such circumstances, the said suspects, of whom I had the honour of being one, were watched and reported upon a good deal too much. Endless were the mischiefs played by the policemen, unbearable to the political refugees—men, like Mr Aurobindo Ghose, whose spiritual realisations were greatly hampered by the extraordinarily hard conditions brought upon them by police activities. Imagine two hundred policemen, constituting a fatly financed department by themselves, spending all their time in writing reports against you, stopping your letters and money orders, setting up rogues to rob your house or to make nocturnal attacks upon your homes in organized bands, concocting cases of conspiracy and murder against you, carefully, elaborately, and circumstantially, thus bringing you to trial in the French courts—trials which cost you much money and anxiety, and which might have brought you most serious trouble but for the keen sense of justice on the part of certain French magistrates then resident in Madras—spreading rumours that you were going to be kidnapped from Pondicherry and taken forcibly into British India in a motorcar, or again, starting wild tales about the entire cession of Pondicherry into British hands, just for the fun of putting these political suspects into the furnace!

Note, also, that, with the exception of Aurobindo Ghose, the rest of us had warrants against us in British India in connection with the Ashe murder case—and a price of a thousand rupees each was placed on our heads.

All this created a situation very like hell in Pondicherry—when, thank God, the stress of the War became too great for the government of Madras to be indulging in costly theatrical performances which were intensifying public wrath and contempt against them more and more, both in Pondicherry and Madras, even to a scandalous degree. For I, more than once, exposed, fully and unreservedly, all these misdeeds of the Madras police in the Madras press. I also sent a number of communications to the government of Madras, stating how it was known to everybody in the world that I was a confirmed constitutionalist, incapable of breaking the law—how monstrously foolish was the police concoction that connected my pacifist name with actual murder, and how the men who were responsible for such concoctions have been declared liars more than once in open court by the French magistrate, in connection with their French India concoctions, and how careful government should be to avoid being gulled into believing the stories compiled by such writers in such enormous quantities.

Meanwhile, the War had been making great changes in the public mind. The earlier reverses of the Allied arms produced a most unfortunate effect on the mind of the Indian masses. It was at this juncture that Mrs Besant, through her paper *New India,* appealed fervently, not only to the people of the Madras Presidency, but also to the people of India in general, to fight for freedom from the alien rule.

Mrs Besant is now reputed to be a Moderate of Madras and is earning a great name for abusing Mr Gandhi more tirelessly than anyone else. But, in those days, when the War was going on in Europe and the Indian mind was afire with new ideas and aspirations, Mrs Besant, while she stood resolutely on the side of the British Empire so far as the European struggle was concerned, wrote very strong things in favour of Indian liberty and against those who stood in the way of its realization. Suddenly, a storm arose in the southern province, a great and wild storm of Patriotism.

(To be continued.)*

---

* Editor's note: The article was never continued.

2

India and the World

The Mother has said: 'Let the world recognize me.' And the world is doing so. The Sikhs and the Rajputs on the battlefields of Europe[1] are only supplementing the endeavours of Professor Bose and the other intellectual leaders of Great India.[2]

The Mother has said: 'I manifest myself once again in my true glory.' And the natives look at her and say: 'Thy beauty is great. It will be a joy forever unto all humanity.' The intellectual classes of the West have already felt the world's need for India. And we hope that our soldiers will convert the Western 'masses' also to the cult of Great India.

For the 'masses', with their instinctive love for expressed realities, everywhere demand physical proofs from spiritual changes. And the 'masses' are quite right.

To England especially, the Sea Queen of the West, the Mother has offered a beautiful message which, we hope, England will ever remember with feelings of love, and the world, too, will ever recognize as the foreshadowing of a higher human civilization.

The journals of a country are a real mirror of the people's mentality, although the editors may not always mean them to be so. The world is moved by the iron laws of Nature. And the thinkers of a country cannot possibly help writing down the actual thoughts of the people of that country.

To England, the Mother has said: 'Take all. The entire manhood of my children is at your disposal. Enlist them; let them fight for you, let them vanquish your foes and sustain your greatness.

'Take more than you want. Take all.'

Love is greater than hate. Young India has freely offered itself for military service. I do not think that anyone is so foolish as to throw a suspicion on the motives of utter nobility and love that prompt this demand for enlistment.

Some have talked of a reward: 'England! Will you give us self-government after this War? Will you listen to your own higher voice, to the inspired words of your poets, philosophers, and seers? Will you dare to reject the counsels of a pitiful Machiavellism?'[3] We fervently hope you will. But whether you will do so or not, we shall never grudge our efforts to aid you. For deeds will count before the gods, even if they sometimes fail to count before men. The High Gods have assured us of life, and we rest content.

India, henceforth, will have only one prayer on her lips, while serving humanity with all her might. And that prayer will be addressed to Heaven:

'Make my arms mighty for service, and my thought mighty for love. For, by such means will immortality be best ensured in the coming era of human evolution.'

3

India and the War

Call it fatalism, or what you will; we in India, have always thought, and still think, that the destinies of all things here on earth are controlled by superior forces of whose nature man has yet known but little. The affairs of cawing crows and of 'civilized nations', of cats and of 'supermen', are all determined by divine laws—the laws of those whom we call the Immortals.[1] The diplomats and statesmen of the world think that they themselves decide the fates of nations. We think that the diplomats and statesmen are wrong. All beings are instruments of the Divine Will and act for ends which they can never fully comprehend. We know this, and we are therefore possessed with a sense of humility and diffidence when we want to understand the real objects for which the gods have sent this grim and terrible tragedy into the fair and prosperous land of Europe. Our hearts are deeply touched when we think of the immense amount of suffering and anguish which this war has brought to European humanity. We have a special love for Europe, in spite of her blunders and faults; for she has done some very good things for mankind.

Why We Love Europe

Within her own realms, she has fought noble battles against superstition and injustice. She has used her best talents for unravelling the mysteries of God's physical world. She has been bold in her inquiries, courageous in her convictions, and high-souled in her aspirations. Mankind is fundamentally one. Of course, there are some silly theorists and sillier rhymesters in Europe, as here, who have been pleased to divide mankind into hearts which 'shall never meet', but the true seers have everywhere proclaimed the unity of the human race.[2] And whatever mental or moral victories Europe may have won for herself, she has also won for the whole of humanity. We therefore love Europe, and we earnestly hope that she will soon be permitted by the gods to return to the normal ways of life. Her pain moves our hearts. May she soon have peace!

Why We are Friendly to the Cause of the Allies

Even the soul which recognizes and is ever willing to submit to the inscrutable dispensations of the higher powers may have its own convictions, its own sympathies, its own choice. And from whatever philosophical height one may choose to survey the momentous struggle now going on in Europe, one cannot help taking sides unless one ceases to be human. The thing is so grand, so terrible, so tragic, so human. It is a pity that men should have to die like this. But the laws are inexorable. Certain ideas have got to triumph, certain principles have got to be realized among men. And man generally learns new lessons at a frightful cost. In Europe, today, the Allies maintain that they fight for international equity, for the rights of nations and individuals; while the Germans say that they are fighting, among other things, for the maintenance and advancement of *their* culture.

They even speak of Germanizing the world. I am willing to admit that, on the side of the Allies also, there are certain people whose love for liberty and equity is of very recent origin—the principal advisers of the Tsar, for instance. But still, there remains the fact that their war-cry is, 'each nation for itself', while the other side lays more stress on imposing German culture on the rest of us. There is no use in thinking about past incidents. In the past, everyone has been wrong, in Asia as well as in Europe. We must forgive the past. There remains no doubt, however, that in the present war, the right is with the Allies. And we in India—all of us who count for anything—being passionate lovers of the cause of freedom, we pray that the side which will guarantee the freedom of nations, which will demolish once and for all the stupid doctrine that 'Might is Right', which will establish a permanent and universal system of international equity and mutual respect—that side should win. This is the reason why India is so willing to sacrifice her men and resources towards aiding England and her allies. England, we are pleased to find, is full of genuine gratitude for all that we are doing for her at present, though some of her agents here persist in clinging to the old follies and superstitions. But these men do not count for much; England will never forget India's generosity and magnanimity. She will not disappoint the civilized world by denying her present ideals when the war is over.

4

Home and War

To the Editor, New India
October 3, 1914

I am aware that your journal is guided by the excellent principle that no patriot must do anything or say anything during wartime which will embarrass the government or make their work in any way difficult.

And, in craving the indulgence of your columns for the discussion of one or two pressing domestic reforms, I hope you will do me the justice of remembering that I was one of the earliest in the country to realize and enunciate the aforesaid principle in clear terms.

Take the instance of a patriotic family, a big joint family—like the ones that were familiar in our country till a few decades ago. War comes and the family sends its finest fellows to the front. Of course, the hearts of those who remain are full of the mingled feelings of pride and satisfaction, pain and apprehension. To make a long story short, it is not conceivable that anyone in such a home will say or do anything which will aggravate the difficulty of the patriarch's work in governing the homestead or managing its affairs. But, all the same, people will eat and drink and sleep as usual. The cattle would be cared for, repairs would be effected, and transactions made just as in other times.

Even so should patriots regard the question of urgent domestic reforms while the State is at war. Suggestions, which, while being absolutely beneficial to the well-being of the State, may still require the mending of certain administrative details, or the adoption of certain new administrative principles, must be eagerly welcomed by the State, especially when the common danger has evoked mutual sacrifices that ought to have definitely cleared all mists of suspicion and distrust.

India's actual sacrifices in the cause of this war, grand and thrilling as they have been, are nothing before the further sacrifices she is to make, if necessity should arise, for the defence of the Imperial household where she has so far been the eldest and most dutiful, but not the favourite, daughter-in-law. India with her intense passion for peace, born of the series of war-pests which had been her lot, almost uninterruptedly for long centuries together, will naturally be ready to sacrifice herself most for assuring the peace of the Empire against foreign enemies. If any Englishman in India has doubts about her capacity for sacrifice or her devotion to the common cause, let him refer to Lord Crewe and get his doubts cleared.

But the smart ones of the world think nowadays that patience and mildness are qualities of the weak and the degraded, that gentleness and forgiveness are barbarian virtues. In former ages, men thought otherwise. Then it was violence and pride, insensibility and rudeness, aggressiveness and offence that men counted as barbarian qualities.

India—so far as it is permitted for me to read her mind, feels convinced that certain reforms are urgent and indispensable for the very continuance of her existence. Firstly, she must live. And life, according to the Indian conception, has a fourfold object: *dharma, artha, kama, moksha*—duty, acquisition, enjoyment, and liberation. Unless these four things be achieved in full measure, an individual life would be imperfect, while a national existence, in such a case, would be undivine, contemptible, futile. Both duty and wealth, enjoyment and liberation, will be possible only where knowledge is allowed full scope to develop itself. Our first need, then, is education. We want free, universal primary education, of course, under Indian control. Safeguards you may put in, plenty of them. But give us light. Let us teach ourselves to read and write—let us have decent notions of geography and arithmetic. But it costs a lot—does it? Don't we pay taxes? And we shall pay more—India will never grudge money spent for knowledge.

Secondly, we come to police reform. What can the government mean by constantly increasing the number and prospects of the C.I.D. force in the country? If we go on manufacturing spies, more, and more, and ever more, where will they find work? And we all know that someone finds some mischief still for idle hands to do. What is worse, the idea is certainly abroad among the lower ranks of the police that some of the higher officials will be much better pleased with a policeman for detecting a new *swadeshi* than, say, for discovering a gold mine! It is all the fault of that love of romance, inherent in human nature. If we have no real enemies whose very existence may be full of dark threats to our safety, well, we can create them by imagination. If we happen to be rich, we can have paid hirelings to provide us with that treat.

Yet another point, which it would not be inopportune to discuss at the present moment, is the encouragement of our industries. I gratefully acknowledge that the government have recently shown signs that they are alive to their responsibilities in this matter. But, naturally, we want them to do more. I have certain suggestions to offer on this subject. But the present article is already too long, and I shall revert to this topic in a future letter.

5

Mr Tilak and the British Government

To the Editor, New India
September 4, 1914

Mr Tilak's letter to the *Mahratta*, reprinted in your issue of the first instant, is bound to have created an infinite variety of emotions in the minds of his friends and his foes, his detractors and his admirers in the country. All the same, there is nothing new, nothing unexpected, nothing surprising in his words to us, members of the Constitutional National Party, of which he is the accredited leader and spokesman. We have always been saying the same whenever there was any necessity to explain our attitude to the British government in India. The reason why we were not incessantly proclaiming it from the housetops, has been, to put it frankly, our unwillingness to please those whose one aim seemed to be to misrepresent us. And, again, incessant explanations would hardly have left us any leisure for constructive propaganda. And God knows, too, that those who reviled us were too many and too noisy for us to attempt any explanations at all. In the face of the present European crisis, however, the National Party—every member of it—felt that our position should be made clear to England and her enemies, her proconsuls and her agents, her critics and her friends, her flatterers and her misleaders.

And now, our leader has spoken for us all in language unmistakable and clear, may I hope, even to those who hailed his release from six years' imprisonment with two special police stations placed on each side of his house in Poona.

I trust that England's chief representatives in India and her responsible ministers at home are not ignorant of the tremendous influence which Mr Tilak's name and his pronouncements wield over the hearts of his many thousands of followers in India. He has expressed all our thoughts, ideas, and aspirations in a nutshell. We want Home Rule. We advocate no violence. We shall always adopt peaceful and legal measures to achieve our object. In peacetime, we shall be uncompromising critics of England's mistakes. But, when trouble comes, we shall unhesitatingly stand by her and, if necessary, defend her against her enemies. And to those who may thoughtlessly persecute us in England's name, we shall say, 'Oh ye of little wisdom, it may be in your power to injure us temporarily, in petty ways. But you can never crush us. For we are lovers of humanity and servants of God—lovers of peace that shall endure forever.'

6

In Thine Arms Again

Once again in thine arms, O Mother!
Thy fragrant breath; and that lightning message
From a loving soul to another, thy kiss on the face,
Thy living voice, the music of thy word;
The glance of thine eyes, the touch of thy limbs,
Thy whispered blessings on the beloved regained,
Thy sighs and thy tears of joy—
These, at this moment, are Tilak's lot,
Thrice happy, thrice blessed.

Once again in thine arms, O Mother,
After six long years
Of solitude, pain, and endless thought,
Self-torturing, merciless, insistent;
Of Love separated— Love in anguish;
Love, whose heart hath been hurt by Time's brute sword,
But Love, withal, whose vision is not dimmed
By the forces of Time and of Space;
Love that can behold from a caged solitude

Through ages and through worlds!
Once again in thy sacred realm, O Hindustan,
Behold thy wearied child.
Force, Life, and bright-eyed Hope
Be the gifts of the Mother to her chosen!

7

In Memoriam

Gopal Krishna Gokhale has passed away and all India is plunged in deep and passionate grief. In life, Gokhale naturally had many critics on all sides—both among those who wished ill to his country and among those others who loved it too well.

But now, all differences are forgotten, and the *Pioneer* of Allahabad agrees with Bal Gangadhar Tilak that Gokhale's life should be taken as an inspiring example by every good man in the country. Indeed, we 'live and learn'—all of us.

Now, what are the principles that Gokhale lived for and worked for?

These are two: (1) Indian nationhood and (2) Indian self-government.

'India—a Nation' that was the *Mula-Mantra*, the root idea, the basic affirmation of Gokhale's life and work. We all know, for instance, with what zeal and earnestness he worked for Hindu-Muhammadan unity. Thanks to Gokhale and other workers like himself, we are today in sight of the Promised Land.

Again, the demand for self-government is not only recognized on all hands as legitimate, but almost everyone has

30

got into the habit of regarding Indian autonomy as an assured fact of the near future.

We are deeply grateful to the King Emperor for His Majesty's sympathetic message to Mr Gokhale's family. It is a gracious act, but, to us, its chief significance lies in the fact that the august Head of the Empire respects the life-principles of Gokhale. Respect for a man's memory may not mean the acceptance of his opinions and doctrines *in toto,* but it certainly means respect for his Dharma, his life's work.

Even today, there must be certain political thinkers in our country who may not approve of Gokhale's life in everything that he did or omitted to do. But may his soul rest in peace—his country has accepted his Dharma.

8

The Fox with the Golden Tail[1]

A Fable with an Esoteric Significance

PREFACE TO THE SECOND EDITION

This second edition of the *'Fox'* is not of my seeking at all. It is, so to speak, forced on me by the importunity of some local friends whom the spirit of the age impels to do something towards knocking down what has been aptly described as the most colossal spiritual fraud of the ages.

It is admitted on all hands that the ancient Hindus scaled the extreme heights of spiritual realization. But I think that the Hindus of the last generation, especially the English-educated men, have been the biggest gulls of any age or country. And we, of the present generation, are resolved that the swindlers shall no longer pursue their trades peacefully in our country. And this is the 'esoteric meaning' of the fable.

Pondicherry,
C. S. Bharati
24th February 1914

*

Once upon a time, there was an old she-fox whom her fellow-foxes of the Foxland detested very much, for she was very plain-spoken and very proud. And so, they cut off her tail as a sort of punishment.

She said, 'Oh my dear brethren, won't you make me your ruler?' On hearing this, all the foxes laughed a big laugh and drove her away with jeers and scorn. She then purchased an artificial gilt tail and, having fastened it to her back, emigrated to the ancient land of Asses and Apes.

The Asses asked her, 'Who are you?' She said, 'I am the great she-fox of the Golden Tail, the wisest among all the foxes of Foxland. They asked me over there to be their ruler. But I did not care for that position. I have contempt for the intelligence of foxes, and I have become a great admirer of the wisdom of the Asses, especially the older ones. And I have decided that it is better to be a humble pupil among the Asses than a great teacher and ruler among my own kind. Oh, venerable Asses, teach me your wisdom.'

On hearing this, all the Asses, especially the old ones, brayed with joy. And they began to speak to one another in their homes and councils, 'What thinkest thou, brother? While the ordinary foxes pretend that they are much wiser than we, and behave haughtily and contemptuously towards us, the wisest Fox of them all has discovered that we, we the Asses, are the noblest and most thoughtful among animals, and she has come to be a pupil among us. Yet the Apes in our own land have been mimicking the ways of the foxes, and foolishly despising our great and ancient asinine institutions and traditions. Oh, what will the Apes say now? Those wicked Apes! The arrival of the Fox with the Golden Tail will once for all stop their poisonous chatterings and they will hereafter cease teasing and humiliating us by their so-called criticism of our time-honoured Ass-traditions.'

And the Asses rightly judged their fellow countrymen, the Apes. For the latter also were greatly impressed by the strange act of the Fox of the Golden Tail. 'Whatever a fox says must be right'—so argued many of the Apes—'and if the wisest of them all comes and pays homage to the culture of the Asses, we have reason to pause and consider if we have been quite right in laughing at our compatriots in such an outrageous manner as we have been doing.'

But a few advanced Apes thought to themselves, 'Nonsense! How can we give up the convictions of a lifetime and begin to respect these Asses on the assertion of a single old fox, while all other foxes still treat them with open contempt? What the foxes do, we must do. And if there is a split among the foxes themselves, we can't help it. We shall merely cling to the doctrines of the majority of the foxes.' Thinking thus, they kept themselves aloof from the new movement of Assiatic Revival.

But the Revival itself progressed wonderfully, thanks to the winning ways of the Fox with the Golden Tail, who gradually dropped her old pride and intolerance, but substituted instead the worst type of cunning and sedulous flattery.

The Apes bent their heads low before the triumphant march of Assiatic reaction, and the Asses put on pontifical airs. Naturally, all this moved the simple hearts of the Asses, especially the older ones, very deeply, and the emotions of joy and gratitude rose to such a high pitch among the long-eared ones that they soon elected the old Fox as their leader and High Priestess, and gave her the improved title of the Golden Fox.

The Golden Fox was much delighted at this favourable turn of affairs. 'After all,' she thought, 'it is something to be a ruler even among Asses. Of course, old age is an intolerable nuisance, and so is the enforced company of the long-eared species. But then, I have got this consolation that I can make those d—-d foxes see that I am not an ordinary person, and that I am as cunning as the cunningest of them all. While other foxes merely strive for economic advantages in this Assland, I have easily gained a spiritual domination, and this includes your economics and everything else. And the Asses call me the Golden Fox, confound their dear, stupid heads!'

Her position among the Asses subsequently induced the emigrant Foxes to show her some outward respect, and sometimes even take her advice on economic matters. All this success soon made the Golden Fox lose her head. Her rule over the Asses gradually became more and more harsh, arrogant, and whimsical, so that she soon began to tire the patience of even the most patient of her asinine followers. Discontent began to spread, especially among those who were her personal attendants.

One morning a middle-aged Ass whispered to an old comrade, 'What thinkest thou, brother? The golden tail of the Golden Fox, I say, is a false and artificial one. She does not always wear it. I have seen her removing it and depositing it into a box before going to bed each night. What sayest thou to this?'

'Pooh!' said the old Ass who was famous in the Assland for his great mastery of Assiatic culture and erudition. 'We older people knew it long ago. It is the usual custom of the foxes. All of them, even those that have ordinary tails instead of golden ones as our leader, put them off before sleeping.' And the old one laughed scornfully at the ignorance displayed by his younger comrade.

The middle-aged Ass did not know what to say in reply. So he went home without further parley, although he still had his own doubts about the accuracy of his old comrade's observation.

As time went on, other Asses also began to get suspicious about the genuineness of the golden tail, and everywhere in the learned and erudite Ass-circles there were murmurings about the intolerable rule and incredible pretensions of the Golden Fox.

The Golden Fox then thought that she must slightly change her tactics, and so hit upon a new device to rekindle the waning loyalty of her followers. She knew, she could always depend on the allegiance of the Elders of the long-eared community. So she induced the chief of the Elders to prevail upon a typically asinine member of the community to make an unconditional present of the latter's two colts to herself, so that, she declared, she might convert the little ones into golden-tailed Asses by initiating them in all the subtleties of the culture of the great Fox-race, and by certain other mystic processes.

'Oh,' she said, 'after I succeed in making their tails golden like my own, you will see that all the animals will hold them in the highest reverence and treat them as Divine beasts. It will add to the glory of the entire Ass-tribe. And great miracles will be wrought by them, such as were never heard of before in the annals of Ass-land.'

This sensational announcement and all the flattering hopes it held out to the vanity of the long-eared race pleased the latter beyond all measure. A bargain was soon struck, and the two little ones were entrusted to the care and guidance of the Golden Fox. The first thing she did with her new wards was to have their little tails secretly cut off and make them wear big hoops so as to hide this loss from the scrutiny of her not over-scrutinous followers. She also made the little ones always to confine themselves to a small room in her own house, and there sit with their backs turned towards the wall whenever there was company. She then proclaimed to the Asses that the tails of her young wards were slowly changing, that they had already become partly golden, and that when the process was perfected, they would be exposed to the sight of the whole world.

In the meanwhile, she ordered the more devoted and faithful Asses to come and offer daily worship to the little ones who were already alleged to be well advanced on the path to the Super-Ass condition. Great was the sensation which spread in the Assland, on account of these miraculous proceedings.

The older Asses were eagerly expecting the great day when the little Golden Asses, that were to be, would attain the Adept stage and the miracle of it all would once and for all elevate the Ass-race to the highest point of spiritual glory.

But the Parent who had more access to the little ones than others soon found out the real secret, and felt greatly aggrieved and humiliated at the fate of his colts who had fallen into the unbearable degradation of being tail-less Asses. He therefore protested to the Golden Fox and asked her to restore his little ones to himself. Trouble ensued and it was greatly feared by the High Priestess and other leaders of the Assiatic Revival that the whole fraud would be exposed, and they would be covered with endless shame.

The Chief Elder who had, by this time, passed the stage of dupe, and become a willing participant in the schemes of the Golden Fox, easily prevailed upon the parent to give up his fears, promising on behalf of the Golden Fox that the little ones would be sent to Foxland and given a thorough training in the great Fox-Culture, and no further outrage to the parental sentiments would be committed thenceforth.

This satisfied the Parent, and the Golden Asses that were to be were accordingly sent to Foxland. Meanwhile, the tongue of rumour somehow spread the entire story throughout the length and breadth of the ancient land of Asses and Apes. The Apes began to heap scorn and irony on the heads of the poor Asses. 'So you would fain manufacture Golden Asses, would you?' chattered the Apes. 'And the Golden Fox is going to elevate your children to the Super-Ass state! Super-Ass indeed! Tail-less, tail-less . . .'

Information reached the Parent from Foxland that his little ones had their long ears also cut off under orders from the Golden Fox, and many other worse degradations were also mentioned, unworthy not merely of the sacred Ass-race, but of any animal, however vile it might be. Ah, the shame of it! How we have been duped! Asses and no tails! Asses and no long ears! 'Alas, my dear little ones! Why did I ever listen to the perfidious brayings of the Chief Elder? Why ever did I trust the Golden Fox? Ah, my children, they will next cut off your dear silver noses. And you are so far away from me, removed by miles and miles of forests and seas.' Thus lamented the Parent, and, finding that the Golden Fox was in no mood to return his little ones to his custody, and that all his comrades were either unwilling or unable, or both, to render him any assistance in this matter, he went to a large-hearted and wise Bull—one of the stray remnants of a race which was thriving in the land long, long ago—and besought his counsel.

The Parent was especially wrathful against a compatriot of the Golden Fox who was her chief accomplice and executed on the little ones all the degradations required by her, and many other unutterable infamies for which she apparently gave no sanction. He had once prayed to the Golden Fox to remove his little ones from the foul association of her accomplice. But she paid no heed to his prayers, and turned him out, heaping contempt and abuse on his poor head, calling him the stupidest Ass in the whole of the Assland.

The Bull listened to all this, and advised the Parent to seek redress in the courts of Law. And the Bull promised him every assistance that such an unfortunate Ass deserved at the hands of a nobler animal. And the Parent accordingly went to a court of Law and asked that the Golden Fox be compelled to restore the custody of his children either to himself, or, in case the Court should consider him to be too much of an Ass to be entrusted with the care even of his own little ones, to any other person whom the Court might deem fit.

This bold step adopted by the Specimen-Ass encouraged many other members of the community to come out and denounce openly the ways and pretensions of the Golden Fox. The wave of asinine resentment and revenge was set in motion, and, excepting the oldest ones like the Chief Elder, very few remained faithful to the Golden Fox.

One morning, the Golden Fox discovered, to her amazement, that her personal attendant had committed a nocturnal burglary and run away with her golden tail. There were crowds of Asses standing outside her house waiting to see her walk out without any tail, golden or other. The Golden Fox endured all this disgrace with much outward show of fortitude. The judge decided that the Golden Fox should restore the little ones to their Parent, viz., the Specimen-Ass.[*]

The Golden Fox then took a short trip to Foxland. The Asses were expecting that when she returned, she would bring

---

[*] Abbreviation of Latin videlicet, meaning 'namely', 'in other words', 'as follows'.

the little ones with her. But, no. She came alone, and, of course, she wore no gilt tail this time. She had also dropped all pretensions to modesty and good manners. She defied openly the laws of men and gods. The old spirit which cost her her tail in her early days took possession of her soul once again. She heaped words of very bitter contempt and very violent hatred on the Ass-race which she had once praised as the noblest, wisest, and loveliest on earth.

She now began to humour the Apes, calling them the dearest creatures on earth and delivering a series of lectures on topics which were dear to the Ape-heart, such as the following:

1. The superiority of tail-less animals over all tailed ones, always excepting the Foxes.
2. How, even among the Foxes, a tailless one is superior to the rest.
3. The paramount importance to Apes and Asses of voyages to Foxland.
4. The basest of animals—the Asses (a jeremiad against long ears, white noses, etc.).
5. How to convert an Ass into an Ape.
6. How to convert an Ape into a Fox, etc., etc.

But the Apes were not in a mood to be won over by old she-foxes. They well remembered their old wrongs, how in the earlier days the Golden Fox used to vilify and mock them, and so on: so they drove her out with scorn and contempt. She then made a last desperate effort to win back the allegiance of the Asses. But there is a limit even to Asinine folly and credulity. They, too, brayed scorn at her. Meanwhile, the authorities of the Law pressed her to bring the little ones to the Assland and deliver them to their Parent. But she had so far disfigured the little ones that she could not dare to obey that order.

So she secretly fled away to the Republic of Bees and Ants where warrants from Ass-land could not be executed, and it is understood that she has started a new cult there whose chief doctrine seems to be that the land of Bees and Ants will become a Paradise, on the day when they elect an old and tail-less She-Fox as President of their Republic—a cult to which she has given the strange title of Foxo-Bees-Antism.

Finis.

9

Reflections

The Indian press does not appear to be doing full justice to the activities of Rabindranath Tagore in Japan.[1] Does it happen every day that an Indian goes to Japan, and there receives the highest honour from all classes of people, from Prime Minister Okuma as well as from the simple monk of the Buddhist shrine?

We must spread the contagion of greatness among the people. To this end, the whole country must be made aware of the important doings and sayings of representative Indians. And who can do this more effectively than the great journalists of modern India? It is genius that elevates the race of men. The Indian ear must ring with the fame of Indian genius. The present intellectual and spiritual revival in the country will be regarded by coming generations as one of the most brilliant chapters in human history. I appeal to our great publicists to identify themselves more completely with the revival. For true is the message which Vivekananda[2] has brought us, the message that we are to be born again. An individual poet is merely a symbol. We shall soon have scores and scores of them, men of thought and men of deed. Go watch thyself or watch thy brother, either of you will soon be great.

In what does greatness consist? Not in the size of your materials but in the manner of your doing. There is a great and divine way for all doings, building houses or reaping corn. When man is master of his work, he is full man, and therefore, great. Greatness consists in putting your soul into the very heart of your work. We are great in the spirit of self-surrender. *Karma-yoga* must be easier to learn for the children of Krishna.[3] So let us achieve all things by throwing ourselves at the lotus feet of the Bhagavan.* So let us offer full praise to those who lead us on this great path.

---

* God; the Lord.

10

The National Congress

Party differences are inevitable in all politics. Divergent interests as well as differences in character, in intellectual perception, and in temperament have made it impossible in all countries and in all ages for any large representative assembly to be without parties holding conflicting views on almost all vital questions.

But when men bring into political life the bitterness of religious sectarianism, or the spirit which ordained the untouchable and unapproachable castes—well, they commit political suicide; that is all.

Again, a deep-rooted respect for the laws of the realm must be felt by all the members of a representative assembly, if at all there is to be any stability and continuity in its activities. But no Congress or Parliament is worth its name, if its members or any part of them should be actuated by the constant fear of some extraneous agency and should make it their chief concern to be thinking as to how every single item of their proceedings might be received by that agency.

All servility, whether of an inherited or acquired character, must definitely be abandoned by men who aspire to guide the affairs of a nation. Of course, it is essential that a representative assembly should live at peace with the powers that be. But it must be 'peace with honour'. And the authorities must equally be made to see that it is in their interest to live at peace with the assembly. Every citizen must be presumed to respect the laws of the state till the contrary is proved. Otherwise, the assembly will be something like a harem, full of mutual jealousies and recriminations. It must also be borne in mind that the chief duty of a national Congress must be to uphold the national idea and to try to realize it in every detail of the national life.

May our Congress be guided by these principles!

11

Patriotism and Religious Differences

It is a commonplace that, to the true patriot, his patriotism is part of his religion. And we find that the duties of patriotism, like the purely religious duties, are often the easiest to neglect, even for men who honestly believe themselves to be patriots.

For instance, most of us do not fully appreciate the noble truth insisted upon by the foremost Vaishnava saints, that a *Shudra*,[1] who is a devotee of Vishnu, must be held as pure and great as a Brahmana devotee of the highest breed. 'All are equal among the servants of the Lord.' Are not all equal who serve our Mother?

It is wrong to allow religious differences to divide the patriotic camp. For instance, there is Professor Sundararama Iyer, who believes that a Brahmin without a particular form of tuft and a particular kind of painting on his forehead cannot be a Hindu.[2] He fancies that if a man went to Japan, England, or America for the acquisition of knowledge and, of course, dined with foreigners while there—for, in Rome, you must dine with the Romans—such a man is unfit to call himself a pure Hindu. He thinks that if you took away the sacred thread from Vasishta or Yajna-Valkya, they would have ceased to be Brahmanas and Hindus.[3] I happen to differ from the worthy Professor, aye, differ fundamentally, radically, absolutely. I think that even we, Brahmanas, are men, and each man's tuft or dinner is his own private concern, not Professor Sundararama's.

Now, on account of this difference, would it be right on my part to obstruct the worthy Professor in any patriotic endeavour that he may undertake?

True, patriotism must be spiritual, but that does not mean that differences of belief concerning the nature of the other world should be brought into the theatre of secular nation-building.

Of course, we must have our religious disputes. Religion is the one thing where conformity is more dangerous than in any other. But, in the service of the Motherland, we are all of one creed and one religion, one caste and one colour, one aim and one ideal. In the temple of the Mother, whoever enters is holy.

12

Free Speech

(*The following paragraphs were directly suggested by the strange and arbitrary conduct of the U.P. government regarding the Abhyudaya journal owned by Pandit Malaviya. Later, the good news was received that Sir James Mesto had seen the wisdom of rectifying an injustice, and had withdrawn his ill-advised order on the Pandit. It was a nice act, and we are all thankful to Sir James. But what of the other journals, Hamdard and the Utkal Star, etc.? Is there going to be a distinction of treatment? Will any Englishman in India answer me that question?—C.S.B.*)

Englishmen in this country are not popularly supposed to offer much encouragement to advocates of Indian freedom venturing to give wholesome and useful advice to the government. And yet, it is such advice that should be most prized by the government. All right-minded English people will agree with me that only those Indians who live and strive for Indian autonomy are the true sons of the Motherland—not those others who deify titles and higher salaries. And the thoughts that true patriots are thinking today will materialize into national facts tomorrow.

Those who desire to cultivate friendly relations with India must learn to respect and, if possible, satisfy immediately the legitimate and reasoned demands of Indian seers and creators.

And the first thing that modern India demands of England today is that none may interfere with free speech in India. Free speech is the truest ally of every sensible government. When you stifle men's voices, you embitter and harden their hearts. And this world is based on the mind: 'Thoughts are things.'

An old Indian writer says that the wise king should care more for the respect of a hundred thoughtful men than the blind allegiance of a million fools. And the first condition for any sort of State to be respected is to permit free speech, in all things and to all parties.

Of course, Englishmen know these things quite as well as we do. But, all the same, we sometimes feel constrained to restate them, 'lest they forget'.

13

Rights and Duties I

In the course of a recent lecture at Madras (October 1914), Mrs Annie Besant is reported to have emphasized the upholding of one's duties in preference to one's rights. And the Chairman of the meeting, Justice Sadasiva Iyer, naively remarked (in effect): 'After listening to Mrs. Besant's speech, I have come to see that man has no rights at all. He has only duties. God alone has rights, etc.'

Now, I have a right to submit that such teachings contain but a partial truth and may do injury to the cause of our national progress which, I am sure, is as dear to the hearts of Mrs Besant and Justice Iyer as to anyone else's.

My duties are based on my rights. That is to say, my duties to others are defined by their duties to myself. It is my duty to respect my father, because I am his son, and he has permitted me the right to the life and the culture that he has bequeathed to me.

In my view, they are of equal sacredness: my rights and my duties. My duties, I must fulfil. My rights, I must vindicate. Life is possible only on such a basis.

Meanwhile, it is the right and duty of the wise ones to purify the strong by teaching them their duties, and to strengthen the weak by teaching them their rights.

14

Rights and Duties II

To the Editor, New India
November 12, 1914

In Mr Krishnadasa's letter on 'Rights and Duties', there is a slight confusion between 'fruits of action' and 'rights' between *karmaphala* and *adhikara*.

He has quoted the well-known lines of the *Gita*, reminding us that our business is with the action only, and not with its fruits. And he makes the *shloka** mean that we have no right to anything, not even 'to the position that we occupy by the grace of God'. I have only to submit that 'fruits of action' are different from 'rights' and that the *Gita* has nothing to say against the latter. These rights are free gifts of the gods, and they come to each man as his supreme heritage. Our duties are merely our humble recognition of those gifts. For, says the *Gita*, a thief, verily, is he, who enjoyeth what is given by them (the gods) without returning them aught. Take, for instance, the right of

---
* Verse (of the *Gita*).

self-defence. Would the *Gita* condemn a man who defended himself against an unworthy outrage? Would the *Gita* say that such a man was injuring himself for the sake of a 'joy' on a 'Dead Sea Fruit'? As Mrs Besant has wisely remarked, it is only the ideal *sanyasin** that may be said to have no rights, because, when individuality is voluntarily abrogated, individual rights will naturally cease, and duties also.

It is difficult to follow Mr Krishnadasa in his observations about the babes for whom his doctrine of 'no rights' may be too strong meat, about rights being 'Dead Sea Fruits' and so on. But his language is certainly misleading where he says that the Vedas dangle before us our 'so called rights' as a mother might dangle toys before her babes to make them walk. What he means, perhaps, is that the Vedas promise the fruits of sacrifice to the maker of sacrifices. But 'fruits of sacrifice' are different from 'rights'.

Mr Krishnadasa's quotation of *Gita* XVI, 18 is, if I may be permitted to say so, a little out of place. For the legitimate rights of man have nothing to do with egoism (*ahankara*) power-insolence,[1] lust, and wrath, which the *Gita* condemns in that shloka. Nor can rights be taken as the sole monopoly of the weak. The strong, too, have rights, as the weak have duties, only the rights of the strong are not generally disputed by anybody. Mr Krishnadasa is a faithful lover of the Lord, and he should not 'unsettle the minds' of those who justly value their rights and know that their rights are not toys, nor shall be.

---

* Holy man, ascetic who has renounced the world; also sanyasi.

15

Police Rule in India

A Letter to Mr Ramsay Macdonald[1]

From the middle of the year 1905 to the month of August 1908, I was working as a special contributor to a weekly Tamil journal—*India* by name—which was published in Madras. In the latter year, the government of Madras thought fit to prosecute that journal for sedition.

I was not the person responsible for the conduct of the journal and so, of course, they sent another man to gaol.

In my lectures, poems, and pamphlets, I represented the advanced section of the party of constitutional reform. I quitted Madras a few days after the *India* prosecution commenced, as many of my friends informed me that keen disappointment was felt by some high-placed officials at their inability to find something which would enable them to send me to prison, and that the police were trying to fabricate false evidence against me. An impartial and thorough student of the history of our times like yourself could not but be aware of how mercilessly and deliberately the peaceful nationalist movement was suppressed in that year, thus making room for what neither the government nor the nationalists really wanted, viz., terrorist violence.

My public utility was thus unexpectedly checked—let me hope, temporarily—and I had no special love for the interesting role of martyred victim to official blindness and police lies. I therefore sought refuge under the French flag in Pondicherry.

After I came to Pondicherry, I was living as an independent journalist, not attached to any particular paper, but receiving money from various newspapers for signed articles. I challenge the government of Madras to produce a single article signed by me which any impartial court could pronounce guilty under the law.

In the month of November 1910, I wrote a letter to the Commissioner of Police, Madras, asking if there was any warrant against me in British India. The Commissioner sent a reply assuring me that there was none. And so, I became confident that the Madras government had no longer any grudge against me. Subsequently, the Pondicherry journals, with some of which I had already severed my connections, were proscribed by the British government.

In the month of July 1911, Collector Ashe of the Tinnevelly District was shot dead by a Brahmin, Vanchi Iyer, and, as though to encourage the inventive skill of the Madras police, Vanchi Iyer committed suicide, leaving no clue whatsoever as to the possible abettors.

The lower police—to whom, by the way, political motives and political crimes were, and still are, as strange and unfamiliar as differential calculus—at once imagined that the newspapermen who had been talking *swadeshi* on the sands of the Madras Beach three years before must be at the bottom of the whole thing: for, had they not shown their bias for disregarding the law by refusing to swallow the benefits of that angelic Section 124A of the Indian Penal Code as interpreted by the Pinheys of the day?[2]

During the trial of the Ashe murder case at the Madras High Court, I could get some glimpses into the sort of 'evidence' which made the police suspect me as a possible abettor.

It would appear that some of the so-called 'conspirators'—the charge of any conspiracy to murder Mr Ashe, it should be noted, broke down in the course of the trial and was abandoned by the government—had with them copies of a harmless love poem and a social reform novelette written by me. It must also be mentioned that the particular men in whose possession these books were found were acquitted by the Court as nothing could be found to connect them with even the general 'conspiracy' on which charge some of their fellow-accused were ultimately sent to gaol.

The only charge which the police could maintain against these acquitted men was that they were found in possession of books published by me! And, of course, I was guilty because they had my book! Q.E.D.[3]

Another thing which came to light during the trial was that Vanchi Iyer was alleged by one prosecution witness to have made a visit to Pondicherry months before he committed the murder. This was, of course, disconcerting news, but that witness—a post-office clerk, who was well-known here as a friend of the spies—was not corroborated by any independent witness among the citizens of Pondicherry. What is more to the point just at present is that even this worthy clerk could not dare so much as to suggest that Vanchi Iyer came to my house or was seen in my company at any time.

With such wonderful 'evidence' in their hands, the police had warrants issued against all the refugees in Pondicherry, making a noteworthy exception in the case of my friend Mr Aurobindo Ghose, evidently because they thought he was too powerful a personality to play such vulgar tricks against.

Our names were proclaimed in British India, and a reward of a thousand rupees was offered for the capture of any of us. I naturally wanted to protest.

But, in the meanwhile, as a result of some mysterious agreement between the British and French governments, a company of policemen, about two hundred strong in the earlier months, was posted in Pondicherry to watch the movements of all refugees. You will be interested to know that these policemen have peculiar ideas of surveillance. They started rumours among the more ignorant classes in Pondicherry that they had come to occupy that town, that the French were going to give up the entire colony, and so on.[*]

French citizens in Pondicherry were openly made to understand that, if any one among them should live on friendly terms with us, he would be sent to prison the moment he set foot on British Indian soil. And, in order to make these threats effective, the British police actually arrested some Pondicherrians at Villupuram, of course, without assigning any valid reasons; and they would have continued the game for a much longer period, had not my good friend, M Paul Bluysen, that true-souled son of France and faithful Deputy for India in the French Chamber, intervened and put an end to their dirty tricks by vigorous and timely action.[4]

Later on, they said they were going to use personal violence against some of us and carry us away by force. A few adventurous Sub-Inspectors tried to influence some local rowdies to injure us. In one case, at any rate, there was a midnight visit from

---

[*] Bharati inserts his own note here: 'As a matter of fact, the question of the cession of some French towns in India to the English was seriously considered by some French ministers at about this period, but the British police made too much capital out of it.'

the rowdies, and my own house was looted and robbed in my absence by men who afterwards confessed their guilt, and whom everybody knew to be the hirelings of the British spies.

Later on, in the month of April 1912, two local informers who were proved to be in the pay of the British police stationed here—the same force that induced the government of Madras to issue warrants against us on the charge of conspiracy—brought an accusation against myself and some other refugees, charging us of a criminal conspiracy to murder all Europeans (of course, including the French).

But the French magistrates were not nervous fools. They could see, after due investigation, that the whole thing was a clumsy conspiracy engineered by the British police, and the *juge d'instruction* said this in so many words a number of times during the trial.[5] Some other time, I shall communicate to you, in full, the long tale of that ludicrous conspiracy; suffice it now to remark that the affair satisfied everyone in Pondicherry as to the absolute legality of our life and activities here, and also demonstrated once again the old, old truth that villainy ceases to be clever after it reaches a certain depth. For they sought to establish the charges against us by devices as stupid and absurd as they were cruel and mean.

So the British police continued to stay here; and I may add that they are still with us, although in a much lesser number than before, and are overwhelming us with the *kindness* of their well-mannered attentions.

To resume my narrative, I wanted to protest against the drastic measures which the government of Madras had so lightly adopted against me, but found myself unable to do so as the local post office (under British control) was at that time openly in alliance with the company of spies.

In fact, I had penned a long letter to the then-Governor of Madras, explaining my political views and programmes and inviting the government to consult high-placed Indians of my acquaintance both in Madras and Pondicherry, in whom the government had confidence, about the real nature of my thoughts and aspirations—in case the government could not be satisfied with the mere legal and dignified policy of judging a man by his public acts and utterances.

I also pointed out that, even in 1908, when I was in the full swing of my political activities, the Madras government had no warrant against me, and that it was very queer that a warrant should have been issued against me—on the reports of policemen whose partiality for lying and concoction I could prove by documents in my possession (copies of a few of which I had annexed as a supplement to my letter to H.E. the Governor of Madras),* and whose utter incapacity for political detective work ought to be, by this time, abundantly clear to any intelligent administrator—after three years of my enforced retirement from public work under a foreign flag and in a small town where the nature of my occupation could be ascertained from any responsible citizen.

I then approached the local British Consul with a request that the letter be forwarded to H.E. the Governor of Madras. That gentleman returned the letter to me, after keeping it with himself for more than a week, with the intimation that it would be against the rules if he rendered me that service. The local post office I could not trust. And, in these days, the Two Hundred new faces of the British spies, and the liberties that they assumed for themselves, had produced such a sensation here that no Pondicherrian cared to have any sort of relations with me—a state of affairs which came to an end only when the spies began to overdo the thing and familiarized everyone with their gentle way

---

* H.E.: His Excellency.

by spying on some of the French citizens. And thus, it happened that I had no means even of sending up a protest against what I held as the iniquitous and very thoughtless persecution to which I was subjected, and against the lies, which I had good reason to suspect, that the spies were sending against me, day after day, to the authorities in Madras.

After the arrival of Lord Pentland as Governor of Madras, I noticed a partial change in the atmosphere of the local post office and concluded, rightly, that the influence of the spies on the postal service had gone down considerably.

This encouraged me to write a long appeal to H.E. Pentland and send it by post.

In that appeal, I narrated all the facts of my case, also appending copies of certain documents which, I felt sure, would give His Excellency insight into the character of the lower police and their happy freedom from all notions of legality and moral rectitude. I stated very clearly to H.E. that I kept my nationalist opinions intact and unshaken, but I merely protested the adoption of cruel and unjust measures against me while I was far away from the field of political struggle and living a quiet but open life under a foreign flag, on the mere strength of vague suspicions.

The constitutional movement, as I have already remarked, had received a temporary check and so I, like some others, finding that I could not render any service to my countrymen by remaining in British territory, but was merely endangering my personal freedom and security by doing so, chose to exile myself to a foreign realm.

The local (French) governors have again and again expressed to me, in the course of personal interviews, their perfect satisfaction as to the legality and innocent nature of my private and public life here. I have been living in Pondicherry for more than five years now.

And, because a crime is enacted about three years after I have left British India, in some obscure corner of a far-off district where a previous Collector had incurred unpopularity (in the 'Tinnevelly Riots' affair[6]), the British government, on the advice of the lower police, issues a warrant against me on the charge of conspiracy; while the same charge of conspiracy previously brought against me by the hirelings of the same police people was, after a long and painfully sifting enquiry (including house searches and all that sort of thing), dismissed as frivolous and baseless by the local magistrate, who had a much better opportunity of ascertaining my life and character than the government of Madras.

I wish I had sufficient power of language to depict the whole absurdity and injustice of the thing. I have heard and read about many countries, and I may record my sincere conviction that nowhere in the world is the sacredness of individual liberty more cynically ignored than in Madras and certain other provinces of India. I hope and guess that Lord Pentland sincerely desires to remove this blot from the administration of the Presidency entrusted to his charge. At any rate, his written assurances to me that the matter would be enquired into by the judicial department make me believe that he is not totally callous towards the infliction of private wrong in the name of public policy.

But I am beginning to fear that His Excellency's hands are stayed in this matter by the reactionary elements in his new environment.

And I make this appeal to you, Sir, who, as Chief of the Labour Party, and as a very sober and thoughtful statesman, wield a considerable influence for good on English public opinion, to do all that you can in the way of strengthening Lord Pentland's hands in rendering me justice, and in withdrawing the measures adopted against me on the strength of incredible, absurd, and unscrupulous reports.

To the Editor, The Hindu
April 8, 1914
Pondicherry

Sir,

In replying to the Hon'ble Mr Narasimha Aiyar's interpellations regarding me,* the Madras government has made some observations which are slightly inaccurate. The government says that I am a 'fugitive from justice'. I am not one. For, I left British India in 1908. And the Madras Government issued a warrant for me only in 1911. The Government had added that if I wish an enquiry into my conduct, I can go to British India when, so they promise, judicial proceedings will be instituted against me. All that is very reasonable. But that was not the main point of my representation to H.E. the Governor of Madras. I have made certain definite charges against the Madras Police and I have tried to demonstrate these charges by adducing positive proofs. Is my presence essential in British India for the Government to hold an enquiry into the conduct of the Police?

---

* B.V. Narasimha Iyer was a nationalist who later became a holy man. Following the publication of Bharati's letter to Ramsay Macdonald: in The Hindu, Iyer led an interpellation in the Madras Legislative Council on April 2, 1914, asking whether the government had made a judicial enquiry into Bharati's case, as the then-Governor of Madras had promised. In a note to the later re-publication of Bharati's letter by Bharati Prachuralayam press, the editors outline the government's response as follows: "The Government, in its reply, stated that no enquiry was held, that the man (Bharati) was a fugitive from justice and that, if he so desired, he might go to British India, when legal proceedings would be instituted." In reply to this, Bharati wrote, once again, to The Hindu.

16

The Coming Age

From the beginning of history, the higher human will has been consistently striving to bring about perfect fellowship, or at least mutual harmlessness, among human beings. The poets of the race have sung of it, prophets have preached it, and even legislators have often pretended to work for it. But the construction of human society could only appeal to the intellects and emotions of a few classes, who had to be content with regarding the higher teachings as ideal counsels which yet could never be made practical in ordinary human life. So the Will of Man, aspiring towards the heights, has ever been defeated by the old animal custom of treating human life as a theatre of 'competition'— that is to say, mutual injury and endless strife for securing physical necessities and luxuries. Competition is said to be the declared rule of life among animals, but human 'civilization' has aggravated that evil principle into such terrible forms that we are worse than the lower animals in certain respects. There are plenty of crows in the town where I live. But I find that the crows do not fight each other a thousandth part so badly as men have ever been doing, and are doing, for food and shelter.

What the Westerners call socialism is not clearly understood here. But still, for the West as well as the East, there is only one decent way of living, viz.,[1] to make the earth common property, and live on it as fellow-workers and co-partners. We have a tradition that, in the *Krita-yuga,*[*] men lived like that in this country. That may or may not be true. But human will shall yet succeed in bringing about that Krita-yuga in all countries and in a not far-off future. The higher Will of Man has been baulked till now, because, for some reason or other, it could not direct the main part of its energy towards rectifying the root of all our social ills. Justice must be made to triumph in the very formation of human society. And then, she will naturally triumph in all human affairs and relations. So long as the principle of competition holds sway over the structure of human associations, so long as land and water do not belong commonly to all human beings, men are bound to behave worse than brutes, in their 'economic' relations at any rate. They are fools, who think that the sages had no knowledge of political economy. The Rishis were wise, not merely in their teachings about the other world, as certain people imagine; they were equally wise in their teachings about this world. When the majority of men realize this fact fully, we shall have taken the next step in our upward evolution.

---

* The Hindu mythological era when human life is at its most ideal; see also the discussion in Chapter 35, Andal, the Vaishnava Poetess, footnote 3.

17

New Birth

Ring all the temple bells. For India is born again.

Her new name is the one that she had long, long ago—the Bharata-land. Great is her thirst for new things. But, after all, the new things are really older than the old. The world moves in cycles.

Ring all the temple bells. The re-born Mother has begun to speak, to sing and to dance. She plays, the infant Devi, daughter of old Himalaya and the predestined bride of Mahadeva, the Great God; and her play is the working of miracles. Her speech and her song send a thrill of joy into the core of the world.

Ring all the temple bells. The Infant Mother opens her Veda and reads. The mighty chants of her ancient seers, intoxicated with love and illumined by the knowing of the Eternal, those old songs of sacrifice and immortality—she reads them greedily once again; and, once again, she understands them aright. For she has met her *guru,* Mahadeva himself.

Oh, ring all the temple bells. Make feasts and festivals. The Mother is gaining secular knowledge. She is learning arts, sciences, trades. Behold her excelling her astonished teachers in all things. Behold how she teaches under the pretence of being taught.

Oh, ring, ring, ring all the temple bells. Make feasts and festivals. Pour out songs of praise and thanksgiving to the high heavens. Proclaim universal joy. For the Mother has realized her destiny. She has met the Great Divine—as her Lover.

II

Social Justice

18

The Place of Woman

In the mystic symbolism of the Hindus, Siva wears his divine consort, who is also his mother, as part of his body; Vishnu wears the Goddess of Wealth on his chest; and the four-faced Father of the Worlds holds the soul of Learning on his tongue.[1] Christianity, in its earlier form of Roman Catholicism, attributed a partially (but not wholly) divine status to Mary, mother of God. But Protestantism has dethroned her from that position and rendered her merely human. Islam, some allege—I hope it is a wanton slander—denies a soul to woman.

Civilization is the taming down of man by woman. Men, indeed, have till now been trying, with scant success, to civilize one another by means of the sword and the bullet, the prison-cell, the gibbet, and the rack. But it has been the lot of woman to have no other weapon than fables, parables, and symbols in *her* work of civilizing man.

I don't mean to say that man had not the major part in the making of spiritual symbols and creeds. But I do mean to say that everywhere those symbols and creeds are upheld and preserved more devoutly by woman than by man. I have read a European freethinker pathetically complaining that it is woman's firm adhesion to the Church that has saved it and still maintains it as a potent force, notwithstanding the mighty strides of rationalistic science. And in India, we know, but for the adamantine stand made by our women, that all our temples and images would have become mere powder and dust by this time before the terrific onslaughts of European Christianity and European Materialism.

The mere historic personalities of Rama and Krishna, Buddha and Christ—which, by the way, have been seriously doubted, every one of them—do not, even among the faithful, count for so much as the mythological or spiritual examples. A Krishna or a Buddha, who was once a great man or an incarnation or what you will, but who, since, has become as dead as Alexander the Great, ought not to mean much for anyone. The object of men in adoring these examples is that they must also try to live like those heroes. And it is towards this realization that woman has been striving far more strenuously than man.

Where woman comes, comes Art. And what is Art, if not the effort of humanity towards divinity?

There is a saying in Sanskrit: *'Grihini griham uchyate'* ('Home is but a synonym for wife.').

Nor is it without significance that the country of spiritual liberation, India, should, at this hour of her mighty awakening, have adopted as her most potent spell, the words 'Vande Mataram' *i.e.*, 'I salute the Mother.' That means that the first work of a regenerated India will be to place the Mother, *i.e.*, womankind, on the pedestal of spiritual superiority. Others speak of their Fatherlands. To us, the Nation is represented by the word *'Mata'*.

But if woman has always been the civilizer and, therefore, the spiritual superior of man, why did she ever become enslaved at all? For it is not only among Indians, but also among the Europeans and the Chinese and the Japanese and the Hottentots, as, indeed, among all brutes and birds and insects, that the female has been content, till now, to occupy an enslaved, or, if you please, a subordinate position to the male. Why is this? I reply: it is because the female loved the male too well to think of slaying the latter. For it is the masculine habit—advocated by an Anglo-Indian journal, only a few years back—to slay those who do not desire to be enslaved by you. At any rate, that is the principle on which all masculine governments have till now been based. Woman, I say, could not think of slaying you under any circumstances. She loved you too well for that. And, therefore, she consented to be your slave at first, with a view to civilizing you gradually and eventually finding her place as your superior.

Might is not Right; Right is Might. That is what Mr Lloyd George, Lord Curzon, and other people tell us nowadays.[2] The question, therefore, that the masculine sex has to answer is this: 'Will you forego the rights of your physical might and liberate woman of your own free choice, as the Indians seem to expect the British to do to India? Or, will you go on tyrannizing the age-long sufferer, woman, until the gods send more of their wrath onto poor Earth?'

Nations are made of homes. And so long as you do not have justice and equality fully practised at home, you cannot expect to see them practised in your public life. Because it is the home life that is the basis of public life. And a man who is a villain at home cannot find himself suddenly transformed into a saint the moment he gets to the Councils or the Courts of Justice.

And the spirit of Hinduism, pre-eminently among the religions of the world, has ever been to help woman to rise to her true position in human society. It has been a long and painful struggle. The progress has been tragically slow here, as elsewhere. But at this hour, when the sages of India have stepped forth to guide the soul of mankind, the ascent of woman to her proper place in society has become imminent and inevitable.

19

Women's Freedom

Ages ago, in Vedic times, our nation produced women like Maitreyi and Gargi, who were able to take part in the discussions and debates of the highest thinkers of the land.[1] But, today, what is woman's status in our country? There is no use shrinking from strong language when we have to deal with terrible facts. Our women today are slaves. I am quite aware that we still retain something of the old idea that the mother must be looked upon as a goddess by her children. But every woman is a wife before she is a mother; and the position of the wife, with us, is that of a petted slave—more slave than pet; she must not speak to strangers; in the North she is not supposed to see men, except for the prescribed ones.

When sometimes we are pleased to give our ladies the benefits of 'education', we are careful to see that the education scarcely reaches further than enabling them to read a few moral tales and 'chastity' novels, and to play some hackneyed tunes on the contemptible harmonium. Cooking is their chief trade, and childbearing their only contribution to the life and progress of humanity. And the splendid result of all this, which we sometimes make a matter for boasting, is that our women are 'the pillars of orthodoxy and conservatism'—which means, they are immensely helpful in maintaining and perpetuating the conditions of slavery in our religious, social, and political lives.

The root evil is the idea that has almost become instinctive among our menfolk, that a woman enlightened and liberated, who can face the world boldly and treat all as her equals, cannot remain chaste.

Now every intelligent human being will admit that chastity is one of the highest social virtues. But, certainly, it is not everything in life. Indeed, no single virtue can be made to do duty for the infinite realizations of a liberated human existence. But it is sheer ignorance to suppose that freedom will lead women to disregard the virtue of chastity. Was Maitreyi unchaste? Were Andal, the God-intoxicated poetess of Vaishnavism, and Avvai, the fearless moralist,[2] susceptible to the lures of the flesh? Of course, we cannot expect liberated women to be passively and brutishly submissive and obedient to all the fancies and follies of men. And, in modern India, there is quite a rage for these blessed virtues of submission and obedience. Inept political leaders, grown old in their ineptitude, are loudly complaining that the younger men are not submissive and obedient. The Brahmanas—our 'gods on Earth'—who have nowadays become famous for making sweetmeats and writing romantic police reports, are waxing indignant that the 'lower classes' are gradually losing their 'virtues' of obedience and submission. 'Heaven-born' administrators and editors of dull, commercial newspapers are wondering why the 'natives' are not quite as submissive and obedient as dogs and cows. The police peon wants the whole village to be obedient to himself. The priest wants submission.

I wonder which class in India does not worry itself about the growing disobedience on the part of 'our inferiors'.

The situation is nauseating. We are men, that is to say, thinking beings. Our chief work in this world is the understanding and glorification of God's ways, and not the enslaving of God's creatures. If any man or nation forgets this, that man or nation is doomed to perdition.

The slave and the slave-driver are equally unhappy, equally accursed. It staggers me to think how humanity has managed, so far, to be even partially blind to this central, essential, most shining truth of God's world. But I feel it as a special shame that we Indians, with our magnificent Vedas and Upanishads, should still be giving sacred names to despicable forms of slavery.

I am anxious that responsible men throughout the country should give the most serious consideration to this question of woman's status in India and do something immediately to make Indian womanhood free, enlightened, and really human—that is to say, divine.

20

Matri-Puja

(Mother-Worship)

God the Father is the Ideal. God the Mother is the actual. That I am one with Pure Being is a spiritual realization. That I am one with the manifested world is an actual, everyday experience. Indeed, ultimately, the Ideal is the same as the actual; but we, children of Earth, find in the motherhood of God, a dearer relation, a sweeter rapport. Nor need we erect shrines for her worship, nor invent symbols. She is there, standing before us, ever-shining, ever-beautiful. She stands revealed as Nature.

In the light of the sun, in the music of the winds, in the soft ray of the star and the rage of a storm, in the loves and hates, fears and hopes, dreams and deeds of men and women, in the subtlety of a thought and the majesty of a volcano—in these, and in all things, we behold the mother of our worship. The land of one's birth and the human mother that nourished one in her womb are natural and concentrated symbols of this all-making Goddess. Womanhood itself is a more sublime representation.

Our ancestors were great apostles of this Mother-Worship. Para-Shakti, 'Supreme Energy', is the name whereby they knew her. In the dark ages of our history, this worship of the Supreme Energy began to be misunderstood and misrepresented by its votaries. Has not the same thing been done with the Veda? The wheel of time throws all things down, and again lifts all things aloft. Mother-worship will save humanity, for the Supreme Energy renders immortal all that reflects her beauty and her fire.

21

The Crime of Caste

'Four Varnas were made by me according to variations of character and work.'

The *Gita* says this, and it specifies the occupations and traits pertaining to each Varna. Everyone knows what they are. I may be permitted to call this *Chaturvarnya* (Four Varna) system by the name of 'the *Gita* theory of society', although it is well known that the same ideal is upheld in most of the ancient writings. I do so for convenience. The *Gita* theory may, or may not, promote the highest interests of man. It was never tried in its pure form, or, if it was, history tells us nothing about it. As a hypothesis, it is one of the best and the most attractive. At least, some of us think so. But the caste law is leagues away from the *Gita* theory. For the Brahmanas have long ceased to make *Vedas* and *Shastras;* they have long ceased to think seriously of eternal verities or the sciences of this earth. They have totally forgotten the meaning of the older and purer writings. They adopt all professions. They are cake sellers, railway clerks, and police constables. And their general intelligence and character are naturally on a level with their pursuits. The Kshatriyas have long ceased to govern.

The Vaishyas and Shudras have followed the great chaos. They are honest, but they are very ignorant and downtrodden, very far indeed from performing their duties as prescribed by the *Gita* ideal of society. And, instead of the four Varnas, you have four thousand castes. And you sometimes quote ethnology, eugenics, hydrostatics, and whatnot, to support these four thousand castes! But, alas, the ignorant masses of our country have been made to believe that this caste chaos is a special divine gift to our country and whosoever transgresses it has to go to hell. It is this belief more than anything else that makes people insensitive to the injurious results of caste. If you really have your justification in ethnology or hydrostatics, then you have been cheating people during all these centuries by telling them a different story. No science can justify cheating.

The sole remedy is in inter-dining and inter-marrying. The others are mere quack remedies of an anaesthetic character. There are many difficulties in the way of applying this remedy on a large scale. One very real difficulty is the fact that many members of the purely vegetarian sects cannot physically endure the smell of flesh and fish at a distance of five yards. But the vegetarian votaries, consisting of both Brahmins and non-Brahmins, can marry among themselves. There is no rational excuse for not doing that. I repeat, there are many, but not insuperable, difficulties in the way of applying that remedy. But there is no other remedy that the human mind can think of.

Sometimes people who seem half-inclined to admit the injustice and futility of caste suddenly turn around and shout: 'But they have similar prejudices in South Africa, North America, and Oceania.'

If other people are fools, that is no reason why we should be such. If others today are thoughtless by committing the mistake that we committed many centuries ago, and become much degraded in consequence thereof, it is our duty to warn them. But we ought not to make it an excuse for failing to rectify the mistake for which we have been so signally punished by the laws of Nature.

'But the masses of people are quite content,' say some. 'It is only the intellectual classes that are always harping on this old grievance. From Buddha to Vivekananda, many have been the sages who condemned this chaos. But it persists. It is in the blood of the Indian people.'

I reply that the people are not contented. That is proven by the very fact that, for these two thousand and five hundred years, great ones have again and again risen from the ranks of the people and condemned this caste in no measured language. During these two thousand and five hundred years, it has lost most of its saving features. Little vitality is now left in it. The form remains with a shadow of life and a million bad wounds on it. Let none rejoice that caste takes a long time in dying, for its life will be all the ghastlier for that.

Who knows? Who knows that the Brahmanas may not purify themselves by the waters of knowledge and then recognize that no caste can be irredeemably impure? Who knows that the other castes which have been out-Heroding Herod, the castes which are fonder of their chains than the Brahmanas themselves—that even they may not behold the vision of the age and proclaim democracy?

If only the Brahmanas of today will read aright the signs of the times, then they will see that Democracy, far from being a thing to be dreaded, will be as great a joy to them as to any other class. The three watchwords of France—Liberty, Equality, and Fraternity*—when fully understood by men, will really prove to be the highest guides of human evolution.

---

* 'Liberté, égalité, fraternité' was the motto of the French Revolution and is now the motto of France.

22

Love and Marriage

The little birds do not hasten to seek their mates as soon as they come out of their eggs. The laws of nature are divine; they are the visible manifestations of the Will Divine that ordains this universe. And it is a law of Nature that the male and the female shall unite only after reaching their adolescence, their *pakva* (ripeness).

The first and spontaneous love of two souls, that strange and mystic soul magnetism which poets have ever glorified as a foretaste of the 'Immortal realms' is Nature's guarantee that these two souls have been made for each other. It is idle to pretend that parents or anyone else can know more than God. We often condemn true love to be the way of sin, by making matrimony precede adolescence and free choice. The lads and lasses will choose for themselves, and often, that choice may not tally with the parental 'arrangement'.

But 'Love is blind'. It reasons not. And yet, its instincts are sure. And never can it be blinder than that spirit of commercialism and social fear that prompts the parents to marry their infants even as young as two or three years old.

I have seen, among 'wealthy and respectable Brahmanas', babies wrenched from their mother's breasts, yelling, in order to be made 'wives' to equally helpless male ones—all the 'sacred rites' ordained by the 'holy scriptures' being duly observed.

Men live long, useful, and happy lives where they strive to understand Nature's intentions and follow them scrupulously. But they perish like plague-stricken rats where they set themselves or their grandfathers up as wiser than nature.

My youthful brothers and sisters of the Motherland, my appeal is to you: defer marriage as long as possible, even after reaching adolescence. And when you feel sure that you have found your soul's true companion, love, claim, and win—and praise the Gods! If any self-constituted guardians of effete forms and conventions stand in your way, ask them to mind their own business—away!

My youthful brothers and sisters of the Motherland, love, love truly, and love against heavy odds. For by love shall ye be liberated. It is the living nectar lent by the Immortal Gods to poor, mortal men.

We live because we love; not because we make compromises. Love is life. Custom is nothing.

III

Philosophical Essays

23

The Dawn

'She widens from the extremity of Heaven over the Earth. Meet ye the Dawn as she shines wide towards you and with surrender bring forward your complete energy . . . By Heaven's illuminings one perceives her a bearer of Truth.'— Rig Veda III.61.

In this deathless imagery of the great seer, Visvamitra, we have a fine picture of all types of Renaissance, individual or national, material or spiritual. It must be noted, first of all, that, to the Aryan* mind, the 'Dawn' is never a product of existing Earthly conditions. It always comes on us from the extremity of Heaven. It is ever from the realms above the mental that the great Light descends which makes for regeneration in men and in nations. And when, after the long hours of the sombre night, Dawn comes forth, the 'Bride of Bliss', the 'Vision of Felicity', 'richly-stored with substance', and 'many-thoughted', you must advance to

---

* By 'Aryan', Bharati is referring to the ancient people who are said to have settled in India from the North and composed the Vedas. The Sanskrit word *arya* means 'noble'.

meet her and throw yourself at her feet in full surrender, in order that she may touch you into immortality.

All new knowledge is 'revealed'. All truth comes of inspiration. If you ask any scientist how he made his best discoveries, he will tell you that they just came to him from somewhere. It is a common experience with poets that they receive their best songs from above. A few days ago, I asked Sri Aurobindo Ghose how he got his new and marvellous theory of Vedic interpretation. 'It was shown me,' he said, and I knew he meant it in a very literal sense. All truth is inspired. The popular mistake is to suppose that this revelation, this inspiration, must ever be the unique privilege of a few souls specially favoured of the gods. But the Veda tells us that we can all bring forward our complete energy by fully yielding to the Dawn.

And, of course, the 'complete energy' of any man is only another name for the supreme energy—the Para-Shakti of God.

All is One. And the purely spiritual verses of Visvamitra can well be adopted as the authoritative text describing the character and the scope of the great movement of intellectual and moral regeneration in our country. Addressing the Dawn divine, Visvamitra sings: 'O Thou of plenitudes, Goddess ancient, yet ever young! Thou movest many-thoughted, following the law of thine activities, O bearer of every boon. Dawn divine, shine out, sending forth the pleasant voices of the Truth.' What a beautiful picture, this, of a great Renaissance like ours!

Again, 'From Dawn as she approaches shining out on thee, O Agni, thou seekest and attainest to the Substance of Delight.'[1]

'Agni,' says Aurobindo Ghose, 'is the illumined will.' Let your higher Will, the 'fire' in you meet the Dawn. It shall then seek and attain to the 'Substance of Delight'.

24

Rasa

The Keyword of Indian Culture

Rasa primarily means essence. Juice, taste, water, blood, elixir, beauty, sentiment—these are a few among the score of meanings given to this word by the Sanskrit dictionaries.

When, forgetful of the self and the world, you are borne in ecstasy to the realm of pure Being, you are said to enjoy the Rasa of Immortality.

Or, again, when a passionate grief has devoured your heart, and you rend the skies by your loud wailings, cursing the gods and knocking your head against the earth, you are still enjoying a Rasa—that of sorrow, of wild self-pitying. It is the lower form of the Karuna-Rasa, so the books tell us. Karuna is compassion and its higher form is, of course, the pity that you feel for the pain of others.

All life is Rasa. Our ancient writers reduce all forms of experience, emotional, intellectual, or spiritual into nine Rasas: Love, Mirth, Compassion, Heroism, Wrath, Fear, Repugnance,

Wonder, and Peace. But they say that all these are one, *au fond.**
As moonlight is reflected variously by the clear spring and the
muddy pond, by the moonstone and the pile of bricks, so does
one and the same Rasa manifest itself variously under various
conditions in the human mind.

What is Rasa, then?

It is the form of Shakti, the feminine aspect of the Supreme
Being. For God is two-fold—Being and Energy, Masculine and
Feminine, Absolute and Relative, Purusha and Shakti.

In the unity of these two aspects, Existence becomes. And
in the manifestations of Shakti, Existence moves and acts.
It is eternal, this play, *lila,* of Siva, the Being, and Shakti,
His Energy. And the wise ones say that she is ever a virgin,
ever pure and ever of a marvellous and immortal beauty, this
Shakti of God.

And, man, what art thou?

Thou art a centre of this play, the one amongst the countless,
the now in the midst of the ever.

God is in thee, in the innermost depth of thy being, watching
and silently enjoying the beauty of this Shakti's perennial dance
and ceaseless music, sad or joyful, aggressive or shrinking, madly
passionate or sublimely calm.

Thou art nothing, O man, but enchanted Being, and
His ever-enchanting, ever-beloved Energy. Siva-Shakti is thy
name—even as it is the name of all things.

Now the nature of this Shakti is Rasa. It is juicy, tasteful and
beauteous, infinitely and for ever.

---

* French: meaning 'at heart' or 'fundamentally'. Bharati was fluent in French
and, perhaps as a result of his prolonged stay in Pondicherry, he commonly
introduces French expressions into his writing in English.

This is the basic theory of Indian culture, the fundamental justification of India's arts and her literature, her aspirations and achievements, her life and her actions.

And, today, her Renaissance means her return to this fundamental doctrine of life.

Rasa, then, is the magic word that has awakened the Mother from her slumber of centuries, that has brought light into her eyes and gladness into her heart.

'What has been shall yet be.' Her music will yet be recognized as the most marvellous in the world; her literature, her painting and her sculpture will yet be a revelation of beauty and immortality to the wondering nations; her life and acts will yet be ennobling examples for a grateful humanity—for India is coming back to a recognition of Rasa as the secret of all life.

All Rasa is one. The trembling coward is wasting the material which can be utilized for making himself a hero.

In this drama of life our parts are chosen by ourselves. *Allons!** Let us be gods and goddesses.

---

* A very idiomatic French expression that can be roughly translated as 'Onward!' or 'Let us go on!'

25

Immortality

A thousand voices have declared it of old, and some are proclaiming it today, but still it is not an 'old truth'. It is very new, this truth of 'immortality'. Many millions declare it, and many millions of millions realize it, in all the worlds.

Man can make himself immortal here on earth by making his personality one with the Soul of the Universe. This unification can be achieved by the ceaseless exercise of Will. Collect all the life-streams and thought-streams in thy being, making them all into a mighty river. Let this mighty river ever flow towards the Truth. And the Truth shall make thee immortal.

The body must be prepared for holding and reflecting the light even before the latter is realized in the mind. This can be done by dispensing with all superfluities in dress, and by a constant and intelligent motion of the limbs. We must give the body sufficient natural food, when it really requires it. We must keep it clean and tidy, vigorous and active. But we must never worry our minds about it, never entertain any fears on its behalf and never release our complete mastery over it. Life can be made electric, thoughts luminous, and the soul joyous by exercising all our inner and outer faculties justly and well, all the while 'meditating on the Truth'.

For a Divine Truth is the first reality of man's experience. There is a Beauty in the heart of this world. All conscious things are conscious of it in various degrees. Indeed, some may deny the All-Great of the Universe while they are arguing either with themselves or with others. But all have felt it. It is what you know as existence, life, thought, passion, aspiration or love. The All-Great is the foundation of the sense of reality. The world lives. It has, therefore, a life working in, and through, its body. It is the life of the Universe that the sages have glorified by the name Divine.

Deep in the heart of Nature, there is an unending flow of harmony. Whosoever drinks of this harmony attains to immortality. Trees, stars, and clouds, the ripples on the stream and the fair maids of Brindaban—they all melt into one joy of life, when the notes of the Divine flute are heard.[1] The voice of immortality shall make thee realize that you are one with the dawn and the night, the stars and the pebbles. And yet, it is this realisation that a man must have before ever he can hear the voice of immortality.

Self-surrender is the supreme condition of winning the universal life. Men will part with their wealth, their rights, and even their lives, at the call of religion. But, when you ask them to exchange their human self for the divine self, which is exactly what all great religions want them to do, they refuse. For the wine of mortality has a terrible fascination for most of us—and yet by flinging myself into the blazing fire of universal Reality, I do not lose myself. I emerge out of the ordeal, shining and deathless. Brothers and sisters, come, let us strive to become immortals by losing ourselves in the Supreme Light.

26

To the Being of the Universe

A Dedication

It is absolutely essential that I should be complete master of my mind.

'But what am I? I can do nothing of my own accord. I am not responsible for a single one of my thoughts, nor a single one of my acts,' says the devotee of a particular kind; 'God does everything—everything, everything, everything.' All right; we do not object to the 'good old doctrine'[1] of the Vedas and the *Bhagavad Gita* that God is the doer of all deeds by means of His *Prakriti.** You, my brother, and I are not at all responsible for anything. We accept, too, the wondrous doctrine of Sri Ramanuja Acharya, that a man must renounce all sense of responsibility for anything that takes place within his own mind, as for what takes place without.[2]

But—there is a very great 'but'. Good mental habits, otherwise called good thoughts, as well as bad mental habits,

---

* Nature.

otherwise called bad thoughts, are the architects of our future. Therefore, it becomes our duty to throw away all evil thoughts, most silently and completely, all thoughts of weakness and error and sin, as poisonous weeds that infest the fair fields of the human consciousness.

If nervous shocks kill a living being—if they actually murder a man—then are we not bound to keep free of such shocks?[3] How do nervous shocks take place at all? Any man can realize that nervous shocks are created in his body by the great fiends of fear, suspicion, disgust, hatred, pride, vanity, and so on.

I am not willing to die; oh, great father of the universe, God, I believe in Thee, I believe in Thee, I believe in Thee, O God mine. Save me from these accursed nervous shocks. Save me, O God. O my father and my mother, O God, my father, my friend, oh, God! Oh, God! O Being of the World, now, even now, make me immune from nervous shocks. Take away fear and doubt and hatred and disgust and indifference and vanity and all foul qualities, away, far away, from my mind.

So that I may become Love Himself, so that I may love all men and creatures as Thyself, love my neighbours and relatives as I ought to; so that I may injure none; nor others, nor myself; so that all may straightaway recognize in me their higher self and their Ideal.

Oh, may my mind cling to the Ideal, and may it so occur that all men and all women and all children and all beasts and all birds may recognize that I have converted myself into the Ideal which is—Thee!

Through the mouth of Jagadish Chandra Bose and many another sage, Thou hast revealed to mankind the High Truth that the mind and its activities are wholly subject to the Will,

and that is a great consolation and matter for much rejoicing—
that my Will is absolute, unquestioned master of my mind.

The mind may be put into any mould, any groove, by means
of the Will. The mind is passive clay in the Almighty hands of
the Will. Then why grieve? O Father, O Father, O Father—
where is there any ground for doubt, for the slightest doubt
about anything? Why should the mind fear? When thoughts
are the architects of life and thoughts are absolutely under the
control of the Will—I rejoice, O Father, I thank Thee again,
and again, and again, for the beautiful scheme of things—for
this grand assurance of victory over death and sorrow.

May Thy holy feet be ever glorified—I am Thine.

27

The Service of God

The Two Ideals

The Aryan mind—as Mrs Annie Besant has done well to indicate in a recent article of hers—has pointedly differed from the Christian mind in its conception of 'God', that is to say, the Universal Principle of Being and Loving.[1] And God appears to us, so we have heard, in the form in which we invoke Him. For the Infinite can be perceived in an infinite number of ways. And among the points of view so far permitted to the race of men, many are complementary, many are explanatory, and a few are polar in their relations with one another.

We find that the Aryan and Christian realizations have been polar, denying each other at their ends, while united at the base.

The one has a martyr for its ideal, the Christ, the God of suffering, loving but slain, triumphant but dying. Its saints are victims to God, its Church claims the blood of the martyrs for her seed. Its symbol is the Cross. Its chief effort is to wash off the load of sin by denying oneself.

The other upholds Rishis, soldiers of God, but the lovers of earth, with earthly happiness, and not suffering, for their watchword, fighting error under the standard of God, but working for longevity and an illustrious progeny, for the joy of faithful soul-mates and the soma-juice.[2]

It worships as its foremost incarnation, Krishna, the Shepherd Boy, with His flute of immortal melody, the darling of the fair shepherd maids, the comrade and charioteer of valiant Arjuna—his divine teacher, and his brother Dharmaputra's most trusted counsellor.[3]

Its gospel is the expansion and the illumination, not the denial, of oneself. Those who serve the Highest must at least have peace, plenty, and happiness. The monkeys of Rama, even when slain, do return to life.[4] The Earth is not for us a reformatory, but our rich heritage. Suffering is the good lesson, deserved by those who serve not God and love not His ways. To the Godly—*Shreyas,* the Good.[5] Our symbols are images of the various attitudes of being and loving, not the cross of pain, nor the agony of death.

The seed of the Hindu Church is good song and good cheer. Agni and Varuna love tender meat and the juice of the soma plant.[6] Siva and Vishnu, holier and higher, are pleased with flowers and fruits. But none of the Gods has any use for human blood, except the Durga of a few extinct cults among the lower classes and certain exalted schools of allegorical mysticism.[7]

We perish not at the feet of error's fortresses. Where we arrive, error exists not. For we serve God, and He can never reward His service by humiliation and death. In His service we enter into a greater, a richer, a prouder, and a happier life. When men find God, the earth becomes a Paradise. Where the son of the Hindu God—Parvati Kumara*—is present, there is no Herod, no Pharisee.† Men and gods serve each other, and truth is adored, glorified and victorious, not crucified. The way to God is not by washing away sins, but by bringing light where darkness was. We reach purity, not by suffering, but by illumination. Of course, illumination is often found by suffering, but illumination can also be found in a different and higher way—by trustfulness, and by straightness.[8]

But a nominal Christian may not have a true idea of the Christian faith, even as a nominal Aryan may be absolutely untouched by the teachings of the Vedas and the stories of the Puranas. The shaven crown does not always indicate the saint, and the holy thread but rarely shows the Brahmana.

But where the two Ideals may be really operative, the results produced are bound to be diametrically opposite. Well has Mrs Besant pointed out that the West is in need of the teachings of the East, and the East is in need of the practicality of the West.

The Bible saves. The Veda immortalizes.

The Bible saves—by the Cross. The Veda immortalizes by *Soma-Rasa,* the Spiritual Peace.

The Bible stands for a life that suffers to reach the holiness of God. The Veda stands for a life soaring to the heights to reach the splendour of God.[9]

---

* The son of Parvati (also known by various other names including Kartikkeya and Murugan).

† Herod, the ruler of the Roman province of Gallilee in the time of Jesus Christ, conspired in the condemnation and death of Jesus. The Pharisees were a powerful group of Jews (though the Pharisee Nicodemus supported Jesus) opposed to Jesus' revolutionary teachings. Bharati was well-versed in Christianity and, indeed, in the scriptures of other Indian and world religions.

28

The Siddha and the Superman

Names are images. Carlyle has spoken to us of the profound poetry lying hidden in all nomenclature.[1] Meditate, for a moment, on any important and vital word of a people's language and it will reveal to your mind something of the modes of thought, something of the historic reminiscences and spiritual aspirations of that people. For instance, a certain school of Western thought has evolved the term 'Superman'. Nature has made us men. 'Let us,' says this school, 'strive to become more than men'; whereas we in India have our *Siddha,* meaning the 'Perfected Man'.

The Siddha does not worship the 'will to power', for he knows that power is merely one of the many things necessary for a perfect life and, therefore, can never be a supreme end in itself.

He worships the will pure and simple—the Shakti of God. The Will of the Universe, the All-Will, the Will not merely for Power, but for Being and Loving, the Will that should, in full measure, be realized by man in himself, if he seeks perfection.

I wonder if the Western school above referred to has, in any of its treatises, described fully and systematically the methods to be adopted for acquiring the will to power. But here, in India, we have a yogic literature which, in spite of many interpolations and mediaeval accretions, still contains the most scientific and rational treatment of the question of consciously accelerating human evolution. By Will is this Universe made. By Will is this Universe maintained in motion and activity. By Will does thought become manifest in material forms. By Will does life stand.

The Siddha realizes that the will in him forms part of this All-Will. A conscious realisation of this fact tends to make the individual will more and more ablaze with the divine fire, more and more assured of immortality and invincibility.

And the Siddha adores the All-Will, day and night. He meditates on it in his moments of silence. He makes it the theme of his songs, his motto, his battle-cry, the awakener of his faculties and the sustainer of his actions.

Teacher or King, vowed celibate or father of a large and prosperous family, poet or soldier, whatever may be the role of life that the Siddha has chosen to play, it will be sanctified by the Divine Will and shine with the lustre of immortality.

But in all that he may do, his heart will ever be free from the taint of self-aggrandizement, of harm or indifference to the interests of other beings. If sometimes his duty impels him to impose a severe correction on obstinate evildoers, he does so with love in his heart, hidden, perhaps, but very real.

Above all, the Siddha is a democrat. Equality is to him a matter of utter reality, as he has seen the basic unity of all beings.

Where Nietzsche's 'Superman' would talk of the 'hero', the Siddha speaks of the children of God, the living rays of the universal sun.

Heroism and 'supermanism' are, by certain people, wrongly identified exclusively with the pursuit of war and kingly domination. The Siddha, of course, is a hero; for heroism is one of the conditions of human perfection. But he need not necessarily be a War Lord. The *Shastras* tell us that there are four types of Hero: the Hero of War (the *Yuddha-vira*), the Hero of Sacrifice (*Dana-vira*), the Hero of Duty (*Dharma-vira*), and the Hero of Compassion (*Daya-vira*).[2] He may be any one of the four.

Firmly established in *Mauna* (the silence internal), fearless of death, disease, and the devil, serene in the strength of God, and happy in the knowledge of immortality, resplendent in his energy, irresistible in his action, tireless in labour, and full-souled in service, the Siddha lives amongst men, a representative of the Divine Will, a veritable messenger from Heaven, protector of men, loving, elevating, immortalizing.

29

Fatalism

Does fatalism lead to inertia, and consequent decadence? Certain people say that the East 'fell' by its fatalism. What they mean is that Asiatic nations have, during the past few centuries, been thrown into the shade by the superior commercial and political organisations of the West; and also, that the Asiatics have, during the same period, lagged behind the Europeans in public 'education'. But we were much worse fatalists than now, at the time when Arabia could impose her culture on Europe by superior force of arms. Chandragupta, Vikramaditya, Akbar, Shivaji[1]—were not these men confirmed fatalists?

But is fatalism tenable scientifically? Is it a fact? Now I am writing these lines. Is it true that I could not possibly have helped doing so? In external nature, all things are preordained. That is everyday experience. Are human affairs subject to the same law? Am I as helpless in this world-current as a straw on the mad waves of a torrent?

I will not attempt to answer these questions scientifically. I shall only invite your attention to the fact that on any hypothesis of the Universe, materialistic or otherwise, the human being is strictly a part of the world. I cannot believe that the world law may be suddenly reduced to the play of chance and uncertainty by the freakish and accidental whims of one of the tiniest centres of world-activity, viz., the human personality.

Man is like the finger that writes; God is the directing spirit. I believe this and therefore I am a fatalist. Free Will, which God has given me as a gift, does not negate fatalism. My will is free or not, as God chooses. Anything is free or not, as God chooses to make it.

It has been observed that the inconscient behave more wisely than the conscient. As wisdom is the supreme end of conscious existence, the latter must know itself to be as utterly a tool in the hands of God as a piece of wood or a ball of clay.

Shankara says that God alone is real and the rest apparition.[2] Other religions urge you to lose your personal sense in the vision and in the enjoyment of God. All this has only one meaning. Trust in God and be free. That is true fatalism. The Gita is clear on the point that whoever says to himself, 'I am the doer of such and such a deed,' is a fool, because, the old book points out, all things here are done directly by Nature. Nature does not cease to be Nature merely because she is using me or you as her instrument instead of using the wind or the waves.

Duty means work, work which comes to me in the most natural manner, which Nature does through me. The word is used in other senses also, as when they speak of excise-duties and so on. I have nothing to say against the vulgar conceptions of duty, except that they are vulgar. A certain human being once made me understand that he considered it his duty to bear false witness against his neighbour—because, he said, he would get some money thereby and be able to feed his wife and children. But the fatalist says: the Lord does all things. Through the coward, He bears false witness. But through me, He speaks the truth. It is my fate to speak the truth, for I am a fatalist and fear nothing.

No, the fatalist, who is still a householder, does not deny that he has certain defined duties to perform towards the gods, men, and the demons also the beasts, birds, and so on. It is only the sage who has conquered the self and the world, who has made the great surrender to the gods—it is only he who can openly discard all duties, always excepting those we all owe to Heaven. For the freest man is still the truest servant of the Lord.

30

Blunting the Imagination

'The greatest crime that can be laid at the doors of one generation by another is that of blunting the imagination of the latter, because where there is no imagination and where there is no vision of a higher and nobler life, the people perish.'—*New India*, February 18

Truer words were never written.

For the imagination—not that of the idler and the dreamy parasite, but the vigorous and positive imagination of the worker, 'the vision of a higher and nobler life'—this imagination is the mother of a Nation's hope—this imagination makes a nation's seers, its poets, and its builders of all types.

This imagination is the way to immortality, the ladder that man climbs to arrive at divinity.

And, assuredly, 'the last generation (in India) had come perilously near that stage' of losing this imagination, and the people had all but perished. A few exceptional souls there have been, however, who, in a spirit of true religion, preserved this fire from total extinction. Did not Ramatirtha and Vivekananda belong to the last generation? Did not Tata and Tagore?[1] And our social and political reformers?

Whatever may have been the merits of the Bhashya writers, the sacred annotators of orthodoxy—and I am not scholar enough to measure their values with accuracy—there is no doubt that the generations of Brahmanas who deified those annotations, led the way inevitably towards 'that stage' which the New India so deeply deplores.[2] They blunted the nation's imagination, and, with their 'Vaidyanatha Codes', and their super-annotations, very nearly cost us our life.

The temples are 'in ruins' and the 'sacred tanks' are filled up with 'heaps of dust and slime, rags of obnoxious clothing and all kinds of wretched weeds', and, naturally, the hamlets have become 'dirty and repulsive'—because men who call themselves intellectual, who call themselves Brahmanas, the truth-seers, and *Vairagis,* the Selfless ones—these men began to quarrel about texts and to neglect souls, to deify phrases and to despise humanity.[3] Even our 'modern education' is far from perfect in helping to kindle this sacred 'imagination'. For even among the products of our Universities, how few are great scientists or great teachers, great builders, great creators!

The breath of life is, however, blowing over the land.

The gods are once again turning to us with kindly eyes and smiling faces. And here and there we have a Bose and a Tagore, amidst, alas!—a formidable horde of philistines, Pharisees, and other futilities. But we are thankful to the gods—for signs have we seen that the Ruskinian 'half-a-dozen men' are coming, who, 'with one day's work, could cleanse the hamlets and drag the tanks' and 'purify the temples'.[4]

Brothers and sisters, imagine yourselves to be wise and great. That means, convince yourselves and, of course, convince others. Brothers and sisters, imagine the Mother as a Queen of great beauty and unfading youth, leading humanity on the paths of peace and immortality.

Imagine yourselves as noble and godly. And act on this imagination.

31

Some Political Maxims

(The following are some of the wise sayings of an ancient Tartar philosopher addressed to Bhunder Shah, who flourished—where and when matters little.—C.S.B.)

1. All men are children of Allah and have souls...
2. 'Discretion is the better part of valour,' it has been said. Therefore, let a prudent king completely disarm his subjects and then, at least, leave them in peace.
3. Keep many spies and pay them well; but never believe in what they say, except when they warn you against your friends and counsellors. Don't be short-sighted and long-eared. Spies are not a worthy class in any circumstance. But may Heaven save you from the spies you have raised from a servile race!
4. Make fine promises with proper saving clauses, but withhold threats. There is nothing heroic about threatening a 'subject nation'.
5. Every *Moulvi*[1] is not a pious man, nor is every counsellor a wise man.

6. Be mindful of your taxes and your army, and indifferent to everything else.

7. Above all things, let your justice be fair and irreproachable. Endeavour to make your laws really respectable. Be very severe to your servants, when you find them writing false reports or concocting false accusations.

8. Cultivate the mental habits of self-confidence and cheerfulness.

9. Be regular in your prayers. Marry only four wives. Believe in God, His Angels, His Prophets, and His Saints. Wear jewelled turbans. Let your manners be courteous and your gestures dignified. Carefully observe the prescribed fasts and vigils. Do not drink wine. Let your beard be scented at least three times a day.

10. Have common sense.

IV

Language and Literature

32

'Vernaculars'[1]

I do not blame the Madras 'Council of Indian Education' for their anxiety to have Professor Geddes' views on the subject of employing Indian languages as the media of instruction in Indian schools. For I am aware that men's thoughts are ordinarily moulded by their environments. Nor do I blame the good and learned Professor Geddes for his innocent comparison of the revival of Indian languages with the Gaelic revival in Wales and in Ireland. I do not know if Gaelic has any extensive and *living* literature. But I feel it is high time to remind all parties concerned in discussions like this, that most of the Indian languages have great, historic, and *living* literatures. Of course, their lustre has been slightly dimmed by economic conditions during these latter days. The English-educated minority in this country can be pardoned for being frightfully ignorant of the higher phases of our national literatures; but they will do well to drop that annoying attitude of patronage and condescension when writing and talking about our languages. The Tamil language, for instance, has a *living* philosophical and poetic literature that is far grander, to my mind, than that of the 'vernacular' of England.

For that matter, I do not think that any modern vernacular of Europe can boast works like the *Kural* of Valluvar,[2] the *Ramayana* of Kamban,[3] and the *Silappadhikaram* ('Epic of the Anklet') of Ilango.[4] And it may not be irrelevant to add that I have read and appreciated the exquisite beauties of Shelley and of Victor Hugo in the original English and French 'vernaculars', and of Goethe in English translations.

33

National Languages as Media of Instruction

To the Editor, The Hindu[1]
October 18, 1916

In the course of a recent lecture at Triplicane, Mr J.C. Rollo of the Pachaiyappa's College* has supported the use of English as the only right medium of instruction for Indian boys and girls. But he recognizes, rightly, that the consensus of Indian opinion is against his view. He summarizes the arguments on our side as follows: 'It is urged that a student will save much time by being instructed in the vernacular *(sic)*, that textbooks in the vernacular *(sic)* will be within easy reach of all classes of people, that an Indian possessed of literary genius will be able to commit the fruits of his genius in his own vernacular *(sic)*.' This summary is far from being exhaustive.

---

* A well established university in Chennai: http://pachaiyappascollege.edu.in/node/11.

Our main argument is that one's mother tongue is the only natural and human medium for imparting instruction. If anyone should doubt this, let him go and make inquiries of educationalists in Japan, Scandinavia, England, Italy, Mexico, or any other land where human beings are human beings. Speaking of the Tamil country, especially, the blunder of using a foreign medium becomes shocking because the Tamil language happens to be far superior to English for accurate and scientific expression—a fact, which, naturally enough, Mr Rollo seems to be quite ignorant of. 'It cannot be denied,' he says, naively, 'that there is no vernacular *(sic)* in Southern India fitted for the teaching of science or the technicalities of history.' But the self-complacency betrayed by this statement of Mr Rollo is quite pardonable in him, considering the present state of things educational in British India.

'Insufficiency of scientific terms' is the next charge levelled against our languages. But the 'Nagari Pracharini Sabha' is publishing a very useful dictionary of scientific terms in easy Sanskrit which can be introduced wholesale into every Indian language, thus securing the unity of scientific phraseology for India even as Europe has borrowed wholesale from Latin and Greek for a similar end.

Within a few years, the novelty of such terms will disappear, and they will look quite natural in Tamil or Gujarati books, even as all those big classical terms appear very natural nowadays in English or French scientific textbooks. Of course, we have no objection to teaching English as a secondary language in our schools and colleges. I think that any rational Englishman ought to be satisfied with this concession.

V

Tamil Tradition & Translations

34

The Occult Element in Tamil Speech[1]

Among the four typical languages with which I am acquainted, the Tamil language seems to me to be unique in possessing an extraordinary number of words that have more of occult suggestion in them than secular significance.

It is well known among all occultists that the names of the numbers one, two, three, etc., which occur most familiarly in our daily speech, are yet potent spells in the occultist's dictionary. But I should not forget that most of my readers may be perfect strangers to occultism in any of its aspects and, for their benefit, I shall briefly explain here what I mean by the expression 'occult speech' or 'occult language'. Occult language is the language of the spirit. It is the language of the heart. Lovers sometimes speak that language, unaware that they are doing so. Sometimes, too, children, devotees, and other innocent people with big, deep, unsullied hearts speak this language, in a similar or greater state of ignorance. But the occultists have made a regular science of the thing; they carefully learn the inner meaning of every word and expression having any occult import. And they use the secular language in such a way that both the secular and occult meanings may sound simultaneously.

When two *yogis*[2] met one another, the first thing they did was to recognize in each other the Spark Divine. Each man mentally said to the other (in the luminous words of the Tamil poet and saint Thayumanavar): 'Thou art the soul; not thou the body, nor the five elements, nor the five senses; not thou thy thinking, nor thy reasoning, nor thine heart, nor thine egoism, nor thy knowledge, nor thine ignorance; but thou art the unbound, pure and untarnished spirit mirroring forth like pure glass whatsoever thou mayest look upon.'[3] Unto each other they made the mental affirmation: 'Thou art part of God; thou art God; thou art God; and, so, thou art myself.' It is on this clear understanding, this absolute and unforgettable basis, that all further conversation is held by the two seers or aspirants as the case may be. 'I am thyself and thou art me; now let us proceed.'

Now, all conversation that may ensue on such an understanding between two such companions may easily be expected to be utterly different, both in form and in import, from all other kinds of human conversation. And it *is* utterly different. In their speech, the yogis naturally use the symbols of the ordinary human languages; but, when they speak, most of these symbols acquire a new value; most of the ideas gain a new import. It is to the speech of such yogis that we give the name 'occult language'.

Thus, having made clear what is meant by occultism in language, let me proceed to exemplify it by elucidating some of the chief occult expressions of the Tamil language.

Utkar is the Tamil word meaning 'to sit'. Etymologically, it is *utku+ar* meaning: 'Within thyself rest', 'be self-composed'. The yogi uses the word in both senses simultaneously. Externally, his word invites you to take your seat. But, in its inner sense, it invites you to compose yourself and put yourself in an attitude of spiritual peace, which alone can ensure any really happy or profitable conversation. Give up all *ennui*, all fretting, all preoccupations; give up all kinds of absence of mind and lack of present interest, anxieties and all the vulgar and foolish and superstitious cares of that most helpless of all existing things, viz., the individual ego. Enter into the peace and happiness of God.

In common speech, however, this word is used as *occar* which is *occa+ar* meaning: 'Get into harmony, set thy spirit in unison with mine.'

'But why,' you might ask, 'should the aspirants or yogis resort to symbolic speech at all? Why should they not put it all in plain, ordinary language, using a larger number of psychological and metaphysical expressions where necessary?' Well, I asked the same question of my Guru. He replied: 'Your metaphysical and psychological words, which will become absolutely necessary, if you avoid symbolic speech, are not at all likely to make your language either plain or ordinary. In symbolic speech, even the ordinary man gets the external meaning, while the internal meaning is understood only by the trained ones. But when you mix up the psychological with ordinary expressions, the thing becomes wholly unintelligible to the ordinary man. But that is only a secondary reason. The primary reason is that symbolic speech is *par excellence* the language of the heart, and so it has become the immemorial tradition among the yogis to use it. And, so far as I know, it is one of the best ways to make the spiritual life practical.'

The Tamil first person *nan* is used by the occultists to denote the third person singular *avan* meaning 'He', 'the unique

God'. And for this audacious monism, the occultist gives the etymological justification that he really intends the Tamil word *annan* which, as everyone knows, means 'He'—but he merely drops the prefix *an* by a sort of occult license. The word *ni* meaning 'thou', is used by the yogis to signify 'Love me', or 'grant me thy grace'. The etymological justification is this: in *enni* which means, 'Grant me thy grace', the first two letters *en* are dropped. *Aham* means both 'the house' and 'the self'.

The word *thuni* has two meanings in Tamil, 'cloth' and 'courage'. The occultists use it in both connotations, simultaneously. *Sappadu* is the word used for food. In the occult sense it signifies unification in mutual love. *Thannir* is the Tamil word for 'water'. The yogi uses it to mean good grace; because, etymologically, *than* means 'cool' and *nir* means 'temper'. *Kan* which is the Tamil word for 'eye', is used to signify, 'know me'. *Kel* means 'to hear' as well as 'to love'. The Tamil yogis use the word to signify both. And such is the case with *muhar* which means 'to smell' as well as 'to enjoy'. *Thol* which ordinarily signifies the organ of touch, also means 'true love', both in the occult and in the classic literature. It is well known among all occultists that the names of the numbers one, two, three, etc., which occur most familiarly in our daily speech, are yet potent spells in the occultist's dictionary. The names of the seven days of the week have also similar occult connotations but, as these are common to all languages and not peculiar to Tamil, I shall not digress upon them here. Again, *nel* which is Tamil for paddy, refers to the spiritual sun, *i.e.*, to the paramount God of Existence.

And so on, with the names of many other grains and vessels and furniture and whatnot! They all have occult significances. Indeed, I scarcely know of any Tamil word which fails to have an occult meaning as well as the secular one.

The longing for the realization of spiritual unity has given birth to occultism in language. And, in a deeper sense, human language itself has its origin in the beginnings of that longing. And the complete achievement of spiritual oneness in this universe of endless moods and numberless objects is the goal of occult philology, which, I feel sure, the ordinary man of culture, and not only the occultist, will be able to realize as a thing of entrancing interest, if properly initiated thereinto. What has so long been the secret property of the initiated few, I now long to spread among the general public. But I do not know how far that public may be willing to interest itself in this subject.

If there are any indications that people take some interest in it, I shall continue to write further essays on this delightful theme.

35

Andal, the Vaishnava Poetess

Preoccupied from the earliest times with divine knowledge and religious aspirations, the Indian mind has turned all forms of human life and emotion, and all phenomena of the universe, into symbols and means by which the embodied soul may strive after and grasp the Supreme. Indian devotion has especially seized upon the most intimate human relations and made them stepping stones to the superhuman. God the guru, God the master, God the friend, God the mother, God the child, God the self, each of these experiences—for, to us, these are more than mere ideas—it has carried to its extreme possibilities. But none of them has it pursued, embraced, sung with a more exultant passion of intimate realization than the yearning for God the Lover, God the Beloved. It would seem as if this passionate human symbol were the natural culminating point for the mounting flame of the soul's devotion: for it is found wherever that devotion has entered into the most secret shrine of the inner temple. We meet it in Islamic poetry; certain experiences of the Christian mystic repeat the forms and images with which we are familiar in the East, but usually with a certain timorousness foreign to the Eastern temperament. For the devotee who has once had this intense experience, it is that which admits him to the most profound and hidden mystery of the universe; for him, the heart holds the key to the last secret.

The work of a great Bengali poet has recently re-introduced this idea to the European mind, which has so much lost the memory of its old religious traditions as to welcome and wonder at it as a novel form of mystic self-expression.[1] On the contrary, it is ancient enough, like all things natural and eternal in the human soul. In Bengal, a whole period of national poetry has been dominated by this single strain, and it has inspired a religion and a philosophy. And in the Vaishnavism of the far South, in the songs of the Tamil Alwars, we find it again in another form, giving a powerful and original turn to the images of our old classical poetry; for there, it has been sung out by the rapt heart of a woman to the heart of the universe. The Tamil word Alwar means one who has drowned, lost himself, in the sea of the Divine Being. Among these canonized saints of Southern Vaishnavism ranks Vishnuchitha, a *yogin* and poet of Villipattan in the land of the Pandyas.[2] He is termed *Periyalwar,* the Great Alwar. A tradition, which we need not believe, places him in the ninety-eighth year of the *Kali-yuga.*[3] But these Divine singers are ancient enough, since they precede the great saint and philosopher Ramanuja whose personality and teachings were the last flower of the long-growing Vaishnava tradition.[4] Since his time, southern Vaishnavism has been a fixed creed and a system rather than a creator of new spiritual greatness.

The poetess Andal was the foster-daughter of Vishnuchitha, found by him, it is said, as a new-born child under the sacred *tulsi* plant.* We know little of Andal except what we can gather from a few legends, some of them richly beautiful and symbolic. Most of Vishnuchitha's poems have the infancy and boyhood of Krishna for their subject. Andal, brought up in that atmosphere, cast into the mould of her life what her foster-father had sung in inspired hymns. Her own poetry—we may suppose that she passed early into the Light towards which she yearned, for it is small in bulk—is entirely preoccupied with her passion for the Divine Being. It is said that she went through a symbolic marriage with Sri Ranganatha, Vishnu in his temple at Srirangam, and disappeared into the image of her Lord.[5] This tradition probably conceals some actual facts, for Andal's marriage with the Lord is still celebrated annually with considerable pomp and ceremony.

---

* *Ocimum tenuiflorum* or *Ocimum sanctum,* holy basil, a plant of profound significance for Vaishnavites and one that is well-known in Indian systems of medicine for its healing properties.

36

To the Cuckoo

From Nachiar, the Tamil poetess

O Cuckoo that peckest at the blossomed flower of honey-dropping *champaka*[1] and, inebriate, pipest forth thy melodious notes, be seated at thy ease, and with thy babblings, which are yet no babblings, call out for the coming of my Lord of the Venkata hill. For He, the Pure One, bearing in his left hand the white summoning conch, shows me not his form. But He has invaded my heart; and while I grieve and sigh for his love, He looks on indifferent as if it were all play.

I feel as if my bones had melted away and my long javelin eyes have not closed their lids for these many days. I am tossed on the waves of the sea of pain, without finding the boat that is named the Lord of the highest realm. Even thou must know, O Cuckoo, the pain we feel when we are parted from those we love. He whose pennon bears the emblem of the golden eagle, call out for his coming, O Bird.

I am a slave of Him whose stride has measured the worlds. And now, because He is harsh to me, how strange that this south wind and these moonbeams should tear my flesh, enfeebling me. But thou, O Cuckoo, that ever livest in the garden of mine, it is not meet that thou shouldst pain me also. Indeed, I shall drive thee off, if He who reposes on the waters of life come not, to me by thy songs today.

37

I Dreamed a Dream

From Nachiar, the Tamil poetess

I dreamed a dream, O friend!

He fixed 'Tomorrow' as the wedding day. And He, the Lion, Madhava, the Young Bull, whom they call the master of readiness, He came into the hall of wedding decorated with luxuriant palms. I dreamed a dream, O friend!

And the throng of the Gods was there with Indra, the Mind Divine, at their head. And in their shrine they declared me bride and clad me in a new robe of affirmation. And Inner Force is the name of the Goddess who adorned me with the wedding garland. I dreamed a dream, O friend!

There were beatings of drums and blowings of the conch; and under the canopy hung heavily with strings of pearls, he came, my lover and my Lord, the vanquisher of the demon Madhu, and grasped me by the hand. I dreamed a dream, O friend!

Those whose voices are blessed, they sang the Vedic songs. The holy grass was laid all round the sacred fire. And he who was puissant like a war-elephant in its rage, He seized my hand and we paced round the Flame.

38

Ye Others!

From Nachiar, the Tamil poetess

Ye Others cannot conceive of the love that I bear for Krishna. And your warnings to me are vain, like the pleadings of the mute with the deaf. The Boy who left his mother's home and was reared by a different mother—O take me forth to His city of Mathura, where He won the field without fighting the battle, and leave me there.

Of no avail now is modesty; for all the neighbours have known this fully. If ye would indeed heal me of this ailing and restore me to my former state, then know ye this illness will go if I see Him, the maker of illusions, the youthful one who measured the world. Should you really wish to save me, then take me forth to His home in the hamlet of the cowherds, and leave me there.

If the rumour spreads over the land that I have run away with Him and gone the lonely way, leaving all of you behind, my parents, relations and friends, the tongue of scandal ye can hardly silence then. And He, the deceiver, is haunting me with his forms. Oh, take me forth at midnight to the door of the cowherd, Nanda, whose son is this maker of havoc, this mocker, this pitiless player; and leave me there.

Oh, grieve not, ye mothers. None can know this strange malady of mine. Of the colour of the blue sea is a certain youth—the gentle caress of his hands will heal me, surely.

On the bank of the waters He ascended the *kadamba* tree[*] and He leaped to his dance, the dance of war, on the hood of the snake. Oh, take me forth to the bank of that lake and leave me there.

There is a parrot here in the cage of mine that ever calls out his name, saying, 'Govinda, Govinda'. In anger, I chide it and refuse to feed it. 'Oh thou,' it then cries at its shrillest, 'Oh thou who hast measured the worlds!' I tell you, my people, if ye really would avoid the top of scandal in all this wide country, if still ye would guard your weal and your good fame, then take me forth to His city of Dwaraka, of high mansions and decorated turrets; and leave me there.

---

[*] Known in English as the burflower tree, among other names (and other Indian names, as well); botanical name *Neolamarckia cadamba.*

39

Nammalwar, the Supreme Vaishnava Saint and Poet

Maran, renowned as Nammalwar ('Our Saint') among the Vaishnavas, and the greatest of their saints and poets, was born in a small town called Kuruhur in the southernmost region of the Tamil country—Tirunelveli (Tinnevelly). His father, Kari, was a petty prince who paid tribute to the Pandyan King of Madura. We have no means of ascertaining the date of the Alwar's birth, as the traditional account is untrustworthy and full of inconsistencies. We are told that the infant was mute for several years after his birth. Nammalwar renounced the world early in life and spent his time singing and meditating on God, under the shade of a tamarind tree by the side of the village temple.

It was under this tree that he was first seen by his disciple, the Alwar Madhura-kavi (for the latter also is numbered among the great Twelve), 'lost in the sea of Divine Love'. Tradition says that while Madhura-kavi was wandering in North India as a pilgrim, a strange light appeared to him in the sky one night and travelled towards the south. Doubtful, at first, what significance this phenomenon might have for him, its repetition during three consecutive nights convinced him that it was a divine summons, and that where this luminous sign led, he must follow. Night after night he journeyed southwards till the guiding light came to Kuruhur and there, disappeared. Learning of Nammalwar's spiritual greatness, he thought that it was to him that the light had been leading him. But when Kuruhur came to him, he found him absorbed in deep meditation, with his eyes fast closed. Although he waited for hours, the *samadhi*[1] did not break until he took up a large stone and struck it against the ground violently. At the noise, Nammalwar opened his eyes, but still remained silent. Madhura-kavi then put to him this enigmatic question: 'If the little one (the soul) is borne into the dead thing (matter), what will the little one eat and where will the little one lie?' To which, Nammalwar replied, in equally enigmatic style, 'That will it eat and there will it lie.'[2]

Subsequently, Nammalwar permitted his disciple to live with him, and it was Madhura-kavi who wrote down his songs as they were composed. Nammalwar died in his thirty-fifth year, but he has achieved so great a reputation that the Vaishnavas consider him an incarnation of Vishnu himself, while others are only the mace, discus, conch, etc., of the Deity.[3]

From the philosophical and spiritual point of view, his poetry ranks among the highest in Tamil literature. But in point of literary excellence, there is great inequality; for, while some songs touch the level of the loftiest world poets, others, even though rich in rhythm and expression, fall much below the poet's capacity. In his great work known as the *Tiruvaymoli*[4] ('Sacred Utterance'), which contains more than a thousand stanzas, he has touched all the phases of the life divine and given expression to all forms of spiritual experience. The pure and passionless Reason, the direct perception of the high solar realm of Truth itself, the ecstatic, and sometimes poignant love that leaps into being at the vision of the 'Beauty of God's face', the final Triumph where unity is achieved and 'I and my Father are one'—all these are uttered in his simple and flowing lines with a strength that is full of tenderness and truth.

The lines which we have translated are a fair specimen of the great Alwar's poetry; but it has suffered considerably in the translation. Indeed, the genius of the Tamil tongue hardly permits of an effective rendering, so utterly divergent is it from that of the English language.

40

Love-Mad

From Nammalwar's 'Tiruvaymoli'

(The realization of God in all things by the vision of Divine Love. The poetic image used in the following verses is characteristically Indian. The mother of a love-stricken girl [symbolizing the human soul yearning to merge into the Godhead] is complaining to her friend of the sad plight of her child, whom love for Krishna has rendered 'mad', the effect of the 'madness' being that in all things she is able to see nothing but forms of Krishna, the ultimate spirit of the Universe.—C.S.B.)

Seated, she caresses the Earth and cries, 'This Earth is Vishnu's';
Salutes the sky and bids us, 'Behold the Heaven He ruleth';
Or standing with tear-filled eyes cries loud, 'O Sea-hued Lord!'
All helpless am I, my friends; my child has He rendered mad.

Or joining her hands she fancies, 'The Sea where my Lord reposes!'
Or hailing the ruddy sun she cries, 'Yes, This is His form.'

Languid, she bursts into tears and mutters Narayana's name.
I am dazed at the things she is doing, my gazelle, my child,
    shaped god-like.

Knowing, she embraces red fire, is scorched and cries, 'O
    Deathless!'
And she hugs the wind; ''Tis my own Govinda,' she tells us.
She smells the honied tulsi, my gazelle-like child, Ah me!
How many the pranks she plays for my sinful eyes to behold.

The rising moon she showeth, ''Tis the shining gem-hued
    Krishna!'
Or, eyeing the standing hill, she cries: 'O come, High Vishnu!'
It rains; and she dances and cries, 'He hath come, the God of
    my love!'
Oh, the mad conceits He hath given to my tender, dear one!
The soft-limbed calf she embraces, for 'Such did Krishna tend,'
And follows the gliding serpent, explaining, 'That is his couch.'
I know not where this will end, this folly's play in my sweet one,
Afflicted, ay, for my sins, by Him, the Divine Magician.

Where tumblers dance with their pots, she runs and cries,
    'Govinda.'
At the charming notes of a flute she faints, for 'Krishna, He
    playeth.'
When cowherd dames bring butter, she is sure it was tasted by
    Him.
So mad for the Lord who sucked out the Demoness' life through
    her bosom!

In rising madness she raves, 'All worlds are by Krishna made.'

And she runs after ash-covered folk; forsooth. They serve High
   Vishnu!
Or she looks at the fragrant tulsi and claims Narayana's garland.
She is ever for Vishnu, my darling, or in, or out of, her wits.

And, in all your wealthy princes she but sees the Lord of Lakshmi.
At the sight of beautiful colours, she cries, 'O my Lord world-
   scanning!'
And all the shrines in the land, to her are shrines of Vishnu.
In awe and in love, unceasing, she adores the feet of that Wizard.

All Gods and Saints are Krishna—Devourer of Infinite spaces!
And the huge dark clouds are Krishna; all fain would she fly to
   reach them.
Or the kine, they gaze on the meadow and thither she runs to
   find Him.
The Lord of illusions, He makes my dear one pant and rave.

Languid she stares around her or gazes afar into space;
She sweats and with eyes full of tears she sighs and faints away;
Rising, she speaks but His name and cries, 'Do come, O Lord!'
Ah, what shall I do with my poor child o'erwhelmed by this
   maddest love?

41

Hymn of the Golden Age

From Nammalwar's 'Tiruvaymoli'

'Tis glory, glory, glory! For Life's hard curse has expired; swept out are Pain and Hell, and Death has nought to do here. Mark ye, the Iron Age shall end. For we have seen the hosts of Vishnu; richly do they enter in and chant His praise and dance and thrive.

We have seen, we have seen, we have seen . . . seen things full sweet in our eyes. Come, all ye lovers of God, let us shout and dance for joy with oft-made surrenderings. Wide do they roam on earth singing songs and dancing, the hosts of Krishna who wears the cool and beautiful tulsi, the desire of the bees.

The Iron Age shall change. It shall fade, it shall pass away. The gods shall be in our midst. The mighty Golden Age shall hold the earth and the flood of the highest Bliss shall swell. For the hosts of our dark-hued Lord, dark-hued like the cloud, dark-hued like the sea, widely they enter in, singing songs, and everywhere they have seized on their stations.

The hosts of our Lord who reclines on the sea of Vastness, behold them thronging hither. Meseems they will tear up all these weeds of grasping cults. And varied songs do they sing, our Lord's own hosts, as they dance, falling, sitting, standing, marching, leaping, bending.

And many are the wondrous sights that strike mine eyes. As if by magic, Vishnu's hosts have come in and firmly placed themselves everywhere. Nor doubt it, ye fiends and demons, if such be born in our midst, take heed! Ye shall never escape. For the spirit of Time will slay and fling you away.

These hosts of the Lord of the Discus, they are here to free this earth of the devourers of Life, Disease and Hunger, vengeful Hate, and all other things of evil. And sweet are their songs as they leap and dance, extending wide over earth. Go forth, ye lovers of God, and meet these hosts divine; with right minds serve them and be saved.

The Gods that ye fix in your minds, in His name do they grant you deliverance. Even thus to immortality did the sage Markanda attain. Let none be offended, but there is no other God but Krishna. And let all your sacrifices be to them who are but his forms.

His forms he has placed in the various worlds as gods to receive and taste the offerings due. He, our divine Sovereign, on whose mole-marked bosom the Goddess Lakshmi rests— his hosts are singing sweetly and design to increase on earth. O men, approach them, serve and live.

Go forth and live by serving our Lord, the deathless one. With your tongues chant ye the hymns, the Sacred *Riks** of the Veda, nor err in the laws of wisdom. Oh, rich has become this

---

* Mantras.

earth in the blessed ones and the faithful who serve them with flowers and incense and sandal and water.

In all these rising worlds they have thronged and wide they spread, those beauteous forms of Krishna—the unclad Rudra is there, Indra, Brahma, all. The Iron Age shall cease to be—do ye but unite and serve these.

42

The Gospel of Spiritual Freedom

From Nammalwar's 'Tiruvaymoli'

Leave all—
So leaving
Render your life
Unto the Master of Liberty.

O dear soul of Mine,
O great Life that made and pierced and ate and spouted and
    measured
All this immense space,
O Glorious Life that made the oceans, dwelt therein and churned
And stopped and broke them,
Thou who art unto the Gods what the gods are unto men,
O Soul unique of all the worlds, whither shall I go to meet Thee?

O Thou great cowherd* that hath wedded my Soul,
Thou that tearest all my violence by Thine illusion,

_____
* Lord Krishna.

Thou who art Death unto the Demons and the Cruel Ones,
For Thy banner Thou hast the mighty Bird.
For Thy mattress the Great Serpent, thousand-hooded.
O Lord of the Ocean of Milk,*
I know not how to adore Thee,
For Thou art my Mind and my Speech and my Deed,
Thou art myself.

True, Thou art me. Thou art the hells also.
What matters it then whether I acquire the high delights of
    heaven or
I go to hell?

And yet, the more I realise that I am Thou, the more I dread my
    going to hell.
O Thou who are seated firm in the high delights of Heaven, by
    grace,
bestow Thy feet on me.

---

*   Lord Vishnu.

43

Hymns to Kumara

The Son of God

whose name is the Sacrificial Fire

From Arunagiri's Tamil Verses

I

SO BE MY SONGS—

Like a child unto the barren womb,
Like a mine of newfound treasure,
Like a floor of diamonds, so be my songs.
Like the wilful embrace of Love's soft bosom,
Like a string of the purest gems,
Like a garden of fragrant blossoms,
Like the River that descends from Heaven,
Even so be my songs.
Like the daughter of the Ocean,
Like eyes unto poets,
Like a stream full to the brim, easy to drink of,

Like the taste of the nectar of Thy Beauty,
So be my wondrous songs of love,
By Thy Grace, O Lord.

II

WHEN WILT THOU DEIGN?

To chase out the Iron Age,
To smite and banish Disease,
To still the fire of care devouring my heart,
To change my bitterness into sweetness,
To wipe all foulness from my life,
And to bathe me in the river of Thy mercy,
When wilt Thou deign?
That I may gather in my roving mind and hold it fast,
And dispel its darkness by placing there the lamp of Thy beauty,
And keeping it ever alit,
May fill my vision
And sing forever Thine immortal traits;
When wilt Thou grant Thine utter grace?

VI

Bharati's Translations of
His Tamil Originals

44

Agni

The God-Will—An Affirmation

Tamil Original: அக்நி ஸ்தோமம்

Lo, He is rising on the altar of our sacrifice, Agni, the All-Will ablaze,[1] and He leaps forth on all sides chasing the defeated shadows of the Dark Realm—the Flame!

Lo, He ascends unto Heaven lifting up His golden arms. And Dawn, the maiden, whose form is knowledge, descends with love to meet Him, the Flame, the Flame!

Lo, He opens wide His jaws, the son of strength, the priest of our sacrifice. He has come to drink our claries and our honeys, well pleased with our works.

Lo, He blazes up, shouting, the messenger of the Gods and the General-in-Chief of their wars. And He has made our life His sacred shrine, this valiant son of the Virgin Eternal.

Lo, He has summoned all the Gods—Varuna the Wide, Mitra the Harmonious, Aryaman the Puissant, and Bhaga the Enjoyer—also the splendours of the whirlwind and the twin Mind-vitalities and the luminous Thunderbolt.[2] He has summoned them to attend our works.

Lo, the Gods stand in front of us to receive our oblations. Now, indeed, there is no death nor foe. Now, indeed, we have found the supreme good.

Lo, the Goddesses, too, are arriving, led by Her whose name is Vision and her sister Inspiration. And, behold, He too is here, the Highest, the son of Truth.

Welcome, ye Gods, take all our offerings—our milk and ghee, our rice and soma-wine. Shining, Ye stand forth, O Immortal Powers, and accept our works for ascent.

Blessed are we and, freed from all evil, we have attained to the eternal felicity. For the Gods have drunk our soma-wine and have given us Light, their highest gift.

And Fire, our flaming priest, has now pervaded the three worlds in us—our bodies, vitalities, and minds. And the Gods have stretched forth their hands for our grasping. And their blessings we have received.

Lo, the whole world is a sacrifice, everywhere the Immortals shine and everywhere is blazing, the Flame, the Flame. This delight will last for ever, for immortality is ours already.

Come now, let us sing: Live the Immortals, live the sacrifice and may humanity reach the good! Live the Earth and live the Heavens and may He live for ever, the Flame, the Flame, the Flame!

45

Unto the Mother

A Song of Sacrifice

Tamil Original: வேள்விப் பாட்டு

Some call thee Matter. Others have named thee Force.

As Nature some do adore thee. Others know thee as Life.

Some call thee Mind. Yet others have named thee God.

Energy Supreme, O Mother, by grace accept our sacrifice, drink this excellent soma-wine that we offer thee and let us behold thy dance of Bliss.

Some chant thy name as loving Light; deep Darkness art thou called by others.

To some thou art known as Joy; while others name thee Pain.

Supreme Energy, O Mother divine, by grace accept our humble oblations, so that we may enter into the state of the Immortals.

O thou true nectar, healer of wounds and maker of delights,

O deathless fire, O source of light and force,

Luminous thought is our soma-wine.

We have pressed it for thee from the bright leaves of earthly life
    by the force of Will.
Drink it, O Mother, for we long to behold thine exultant dance
    and sing ourselves into gods.
The demons of fear and sorrow, with their legions of beggarly
    cares and pains and deaths, do ever encircle us.
They are plotting to rob us of the nectar pot.
Day and night they are assailing this fortressed city of a million
    halls, this Body which thou hast given to us.
They are damming the River of Life.
They are shelling our beautiful domes of the Mind.
Mother, we sing thy praises. Protect us, dispelling our foes.

For our laws, our arts and works,
Our shrines and homes and dear ones,
Our herds and flocks, our pastures and fields,
We beg thy mighty protection, O Mother.

On our lives and loves and songs,
Our dreams and willings and acts,
We invoke thy blessings.
We offer thee our all. We kiss thy lotus feet. We surrender.
Make us immortal, O Mother.

46

Lakshmi

The Goddess of Wealth

An Affirmation

Tamil Original: லீமிதேவி – சரண்புகுதல்

Come, let us affirm the Energy of Vishnu, the Jewel of the
    Crimson Flower, and end this want,
Where the mind ever struggles in the fumes of paltriness,
And Reason so faints that the noblest truths do but vex her.
We can endure this no more.
So let us take refuge in the feet of the Mother, Lakshmi.

The discourtesies of the low, the kinship with those who have
    failed;
The extinction of endeavours like lamps that are drowned in
    a well;
The denial of fruits even when the seven seas are crossed;

To such things does want subject us, this worst of Earth's
    tyrannies;
Down with it.

She is born of the inner Ocean of Milk;
She is sweet like the nectar of Heaven, twin-born with her;
And her shining feet repose aptly on lotus petals.
Multiple riches she holds in her hands, which are four, the
    Goddess whose eyes are gleaming azure;
Ruddy her form and verdant is her love.
Seated beside Love, in Heaven, on the bosom of Vishnu
Himself, on the Earth her dwellings are many.

We find her revealed
In the festooned halls of marriage;
Amid flocks, and in jewelled palaces;
In the hero's arm, in the sweating toil of labour,
And ay! On the crown of knowledge,
Extending the light of her bounties.

Come, let us sing her praises, bless her feet, and climb the
    heights of power;
Behold her in gold and in gems, in flower and incense;
In the lamp and the virgin's smile;
In luxuriant woodlands, groves and fields,
In the Will that dares,
And in royal lineaments.

And firm let us seat her in our minds and speech,
She who is revealed
In underground mines,

And the slopes of the hills, and depths of the seas;
In the righteous sacrifice;
In fame, and in talent, and novelty;
In statue and portrait, in song and in dance.

Dedicate unto her grace all knowledge that you have;
Attain to her splendours, and vanquish dire want;
Rise high in the world by joyous affirmation of Lakshmi who is
    revealed
In conquering armies and the traffic of the far-sighted.
In self-control, and ay! In the harmonious lays of her poet-
    votaries.

Come, let us affirm the Energy of Vishnu, the Jewel of the
    Crimson Flower!

47

In Each Other's Arms

Tamil Original: கண்ணம்மா—என் காதலி (யோகம்)

(*In the following verses the Supreme Divinity, styled here 'Krishna',
is imaged as the beloved woman, and the human soul as the lover.—
C.S.B.*)

Thou to me the flowing Light,
And I to thee, discerning sight;
Honied blossom thou to me,
Bee enchanted I to thee:
O Heavenly Lamp with shining ray,
O Krishna, Love, O nectar-spray,
With falt'ring tongue and words that pant
Thy glories, here, I strive to chant.

Thou to me the Harp of gold,
And I to thee the finger bold;
Necklace shining thou to me,
New-set Diamond I to thee:

O mighty queen with splendour rife,
O Krishna, Love, O well of life,
Thine eyes do shed their light on all,
Wherev'r I turn, their beams do fall.

Rain that singeth, thou to me,
Peacock dancing, I to thee;
Thou to me the juice of grape,
And I to thee the cup agape:
O Spotless Beauty, Krishna bright,
Perennial fount of deep delight,
O Love, they face hath grace divine,
For there the deathless Truth doth shine.

Silver Moonlight thou to me,
Exulting Ocean I to thee;
Thou, the basic harmony
And I the Song that moveth free:
Dear as eyesight, Krishna mine,
O massed-up, sweet, immortal Wine,
Unceasing yearns my mind to scan
Thy endless charm, but never can.

Inlaid perfume thou to me,
Petalled blossom I to thee:
Thou to me the inner Thought,
And I to thee the Word it wrought;
O honeyed Hope, O Krishna fair,
O Joy, o'erflowing everywhere,
O Star of love, do teach me, pray,
To sing thy praise in fitting lay.

Deep Attraction thou to me,
Living Magnet I to thee;
Thou to me the Veda pure
And I to thee the Knowledge sure;
Voice vibrant of the world's desire,
O Krishna, Love, all-quickening Fire,
In utter stillness, here, I see
Thy face that yieldeth ecstasy.

As Life to Pulse, and Gold to rings,
As star to planet, Soul to things,
So Krishna, Love, art thou to me,
Thou, the Force, I, Victory; --
And all the joys of Heaven and Earth
In thee, O Krishna, have their birth,
Eternal glory, endless Might
O Heart of Mine, O Light, O Light!

48

Krishna

My Mother

Tamil Original: கண்ணன் — என் தாய்

(As in the preceding poem, Bharati writes here about Krishna, here in the form of the mother.)

The Realms of Life are her bounteous breasts; and consciousness, her milk of endless delight, which she yieldeth into my lips unasked; such grace is my Mother's.

They call her Krishna. Ah, she has clasped me in fond embrace with her arms of ethereal space! And, placing me on her lap of Earth, she loves to tell me endless stories, strange and mysterious.

And some of the tales I call by the name of pleasures, evolutions, victories. Yet others come to me as pains, defeats and falls; stories, all these, that my Mother recounts to suit my various moods and stages, lovingly told, ever entrancing.

And many are the wondrous toys and dolls which my Mother showeth me:

There is one that is named the Moon, and it sheds a nectar-like flood of light. And there are herds and herds of clouds, many-coloured toys, yielding rain. There's the Sun, too, foremost of my playthings, the beauty of whose face I have no words to depict.

Toys, toys, toys.

A heavenful of stars, sparkling like tiny gems. Many a time, but in vain, have I essayed to count them all. And then those green hills, that never stir from their places, silent toys, offering speechless play.

Rivers and rivulets, fair and playful, that wander all over the land and, in the end, flow into that marvellous toy, yon ocean, wide and boundless-seeming, with dashing billows, spouts of spray and its long, continuous chant wherein my Mother's name is ever sounded: Om, Om, O . . . M.

Groves and gardens, abounding in many-hued gems of flowers; and delicious fruits hanging on the trees, strong in essence, rich in form. Ah, the world is full of such exquisite playthings. All these, my Mother has given me.

Nice things to eat and songs all sweetness to hear, and companions gifted, like me, with minds, to play with and become one with; and these fair girls, enkindling love, that passion of flaming delight like fiery nectar, killing-sweet.

Yet more playmates:

The winged birds, the beasts that walk the earth, and countless fishes of many and many a kind, there, in that thundering Sea.

What a tale of raptures, too many even to think of!

And endless sciences and arts she has ordained and, nobler than all these, divine wisdom—for my serious hours.

But when the lighter mood is on me, and I would fain laugh and be merry, many are the jokes she has planned to amuse me with: the lies of priests, the comic feats of kings, the hypocrisies of age and the silly cares of youth.

Whatever I demand, she gives, my Mother. Aye, she hastens with gifts, ere I tell her I'd like to have them.

With high grace does she protect me, and says she will make me a yogin, like Arjun, my brother in race.

Always and in all places, my work shall be to sing of the bounteous love of my Mother.

And a long and shining life and other matchless glories, she will grant me as reward—Krishna, my Mother.

49

The 'Kummi' of Women's Freedom

Tamil Original: பெண்கள் விடுதலைக் கும்மி

(The 'Kummi' dance is perhaps peculiar to Southern India and is danced by women in a circle. The song that accompanies this very picturesque dance is also called 'Kummi'.—C.S.B.)

We sing the joys of freedom;
In gladness we sing.
And He that shineth in the soul as Light shines in the
    eye, even He is our Strength.

Dance the Kummi, beat the measure;
Let this land of the Tamils ring with our dance.
For now we are rid of all evil shades;
We've seen the Good.

Gone are they who said to woman: 'Thou shalt not
    open the Book of Knowledge.'

And the strange ones who boasted saying:
'We will immure these women in our homes'—
To-day they hang down their heads.

Dance the Kummi, beat the measure.
Let this land of the Tamils ring with our dance.
For now we are rid of all evil shades;
We've seen the Good.

The life of the beast that is beaten, tamed and tied down,
Fain would they lay it on us in the house; but we
    scornfully baffled them.
Dance the Kummi, beat the measure.

The dog they sell for a price, nor ever consult his will.
Nigh to his state had they brought us—would rather
    they had killed us at a blow—
But infamy seized them.
Dance the Kummi, beat the measure.

And they talk of wedded faith;
Good; let it be binding on both.
But the custom that *forced* us to wed, we've cast it
    down and trampled it under foot;
Dance the Kummi, beat the measure.

To rule the realms and make the laws
We have arisen;
Nor shall it be said that woman lags behind man in the
    knowledge that he attaineth.
Dance the Kummi, beat the measure.

To know the Truth and do the Right,
Willing we come;
Food we'll give you; we'll also give a race of immortals.
Dance the Kummi, beat the measure.

VII

From Bharati's Journal

50

Toil, Toil, Toil

O Supreme Mother of the Universe,
Give me the power to work for twenty-four hours a day—or—
     or—but no!
Protect me, Lord—in brilliant, electric work,
     put the mind in pure, ceaseless joy;
Oh, but still, let me have the might
To toil away when the need may rise
For high endeavour, long vigil, and much endurance—
And then, O Supreme Mother of the Worlds!
As doth the active machine toil
Without a break, without respite.
In fullest rhythm, but with deep intent—
With never a fault, never a blot,
So let me toil away—
High Mother of the Universe—
Prejudice and folly and most silly fear
And vanity and pride and all the brood
Of hellish illusions may come to stop my work—
But let my hand work like the machine electric—

My mind being full of Thy holy feet,
Thus, O Sacred Mother of the Worlds,
Let me work.

51

Thoughts

I

I can think like a God; I ought to act like one.
I do not crave for things. I am the world's master, not it mine.
Those things which Nature brings in my way, I take and feel content. I crave not, for the world sufficeth not unto me.
He who writes for others, affects.
He is a slave who receives favours.
He sells himself who asks.
Forgetfulness is the bane of life (Muhammad).
If you want to die soon, talk about yourself.
If you want to make your lives sublime, do good to others.
By the deepest abysses do rise the tallest precipices.
In hours of exultation remember hours of pain, and act soberly.
Be ever working, calmly, cheerfully, but never get dizzy.
There is a difference between intellectual comprehension and seeing. Intellectual comprehension gives you vain pride and impotence. The seeing gives you tremendous power.
What is the object of life?

Philosophy has an answer—many answers.

Science has an answer—many answers.

I have a counter-question:

what is the object of non-life?

I am convinced that *God is* and *God alone is.*

II

On Reason's Plane

We know that the Universe is Being. We guess it is infinite. We cannot comprehend Infinity.

Mind is one phase of Existence. We are aware of a mental life. As Experience is the sole proof of things, we require no further proof for the existence of the mind. This mind, we infer, has many phases and almost infinite potentialities. We have learnt this, again, by experience.

We infer that all existence is one. We have almost proved it by comparative science. We therefore can identify our being with the Universal Being.

We know nothing more of God.

Passions subdued indicate Power and lead to Peace.

Live and let live.

Enjoyment of good things in life is not wrong, but what is wrong is the getting enslaved to them. Getting enslaved to things clouds the Reason, and Reason is man's highest faculty.

The mystic books are of value where they deal with ordinary things and cease to be mystic.

Three-fourths of the spiritualities trumpeted among men have been proved to be ways of earning money, practised by clever scoundrels or self-deluded charlatans.

There is more spirituality outside your temples than in them.

A reasoning life is not necessarily opposed to a life of Peace. Reasoning is not the endless quibbling and hair-splitting of the professional logicians and critics. These are abusers of Reason.

III

Mantras on the Plane of Will

1

That man is diviner than his brother whose wills are fewer.

Success is the result of concentration, and concentration means the contraction of the area on which our will is exercised.

The contraction of the personal Will permits in the being we call 'man', the expansion of what we may call the impersonal Will.

The All, of which we form parts, must certainly have a Will of its own. Otherwise the All could not be so full of acts. And what is the Universe but a harmonious and endless series of acts?

The Will is independent of Reasoning; it can even be independent of the realm which we ordinarily speak of as consciousness.

2

'Where there is a Will, there is a way.'

But, oh, Heavens! Where is the way to get a Will?

Instinct replies, 'In Thyself.'

Yes, in myself, in myself, in myself.

I will that I develop a powerful Will.

I have willed it.

I have willed that what I will, I will achieve. I have willed to will anything.

I will, Will, Will, Will . . . this is my mantra.[1]

I will be strong.
I will grow into strength, I will age into youth.

I will work for Power and Greatness.
I will achieve glory.
I will annihilate the miseries of man.
I will make mankind happier.
I will make the world better.
I will wed Truth and Power. Oh, Heavens!
Grant unto me Truth and Power.

I will work, work, work, work, work.
Toil, toil, toil . . . Toil, yes, toil
Shall be my strength, toil, my pleasure,
Toil my rule, and toil shall be my Way;
Toil my Will, toil my weapon,
And toil shall be my Glory;
Toil my charm, toil my use,
And toil shall be my custom;
Toil my fort, toil my ground, and toil shall be my play.
Toil shall be my faith, toil my scripture, toil my code,
And toil shall be my mate.
Ever toil ever success; ever toil
Ever success . . . I succeed,
I succeed, I succeed, I succeed . . .

3

Success my law, success my Way.
And success shall be my Bride.
Success my Glory, success my pride,
Success my tune, success my lay,
And success shall be my faith,
Success my doctrine, success my code,
Success my vehicle, success my road.
Success my custom, success my mode,
Success my life and my death.[2]
Success my religion, success my Heaven,
Success my only God.
Success, success . . . success!
I Succeed.

IV

Mantras on the Plane of Self

1

I am God, I am God, I am God.
I am prosperous beyond all expectations, for I am God.
I am prosperous. There is money about me in infinite quantities.
I am beginning to utilize all that.
I am wealthy. I am a Prince, for I am God. I am greater than all princes, for I am *myself* and I am God.

2

I am healthy, I am strong, the limbs of my body have received my Godly strength and power. They are agile, they are elastic, they are full of ease and power.

All disease has gone out of my body, has gone out into nothing. I am Ease, I am Strength, I am Health. The devil is weak. Weakness is weak. 'Nothing' is weak. But I am God, I am Power. I am All Things. How can I be weak?

Oh, the pleasure of being strong, healthy and powerful! Oh, the joy of divinity! I am divine. So I am infinitely healthy. My eyes, my nose, my mouth, my chest, my hands, my stomach, my legs, my feet, all, all is healthy.

My brain is health incarnate. My mind is free from disease. Ay, my mind is free from all germs of filth and disease. I have thrown out all filth and disease, yes, thrown out all filth and disease, yes, thrown out into nothing.

I am Health.

3

I am God, I am God, I am God. I am Immortal. The hours may pass, the days may roll, the seasons change, and the years die away, but I change not. I am firm, fixed, ever alive, ever real, ever happy. I do believe in all this, for I know all this to be true.

I know myself to be Immortal, because I am God.

I 'open myself ever to the inflow of the spirit of God'. That is, I open myself unto Myself. I am filled with Myself. I am filled with God. Immortality is ever tingling in my veins. It makes my blood pure and racy. It has endowed me with a great vigour.

I am ever vigorous, ever alert, ever active, ever loving, ever living. Oh, why am I so full of joy? Because I am God.

I am ever youthful. I age not. Ay, even my body shall ever remain young, because it is filled with the deathless spirit of my Divinity. I shall not die. I have no death. No, not even this body shall know death.

How can my body die, when it knows no illness? How can it die, when it is ever recuperated, ever refreshed, ever quickened by the deathless Me? How can it die, when I am God? Do the gods die? They do not.

சந்ததமு வேத மொழி யாதொன்று பற்றினது
தான் வந்து முற்று மெனலால்
ஜகமீதிருந்தாலு மரணமுண்டென்பது
ஸதாநிஷ்டன் நினைவதில்லை.[3]

And I am a *Sada-Nishta*.[4] Hence I cannot conceive of death. I can only think of an endless joy, the joy of existence. And this joy is mine for ever and for ever.

I manifest myself—I manifest myself through my Body and my Mind.

This Body shall be seen—recognized as that of a God. It is so seen, so recognized. My will shall be the Law of the World. For am I not God?

Whatsoever thy mind shall cling to, that will be achieved in thee. And so the ever harmonious ones never feel that there is death for them even if they remain on Earth.

My body shall shine with the splendour of divinity. It does so shine even now. To all, to all.

My will shall prevail in all things.

It does so prevail even now. It has always been so—it shall ever be so.

My will be done on Earth, as it is in Heaven. For I am going to convert this Earth into Heaven. I am doing it now. And is not this Earth a beautiful Heaven? I find it so; and all shall so find it, who think with me. All will find it so, who obey my Will. For my Will is everybody's will. I am God, sing on, I am God, I am God.

My messages shall be listened to with avidity and men shall obey them with all their might. For I am God.

My messages are God's messages. I am the brother of Krishna and Buddha, Jesus and Muhammad. Ay, they are all rays of the great Sun, which is Myself. I am God, I am God, I am God.

4

I am the Father, I am the Son, I am the Holy Ghost.
I am the stars, the suns, and the planets. I am the four *lokas*.[5] I transcend the four.
I am all the subtle things. I am all the blisses.
I am the moralities, the laws, the ways.
I am the religions, the creeds and the sects. I am All. I am All.
I am Rain, I am Air, I am Fire, I am Earth, I am All.
I am the clouds, the flash of the lightning, the clap of the thunder.
I am God, I am God, I am God.
So, I direct and the world obeys.
So, I direct and the planets march.
So, I direct and the gods shout for joy.
I see all subtle existences. For I am They.
I have faith in myself.

I have no need of prayer. Action is my prayer. Incessant meditation on the Highest has become my nature, for the Highest is Me. How can I help meditating on it?

There is no Higher Self or Lower Self. All is the Brahman.

'The Spirit of Infinite Life and Power that animates all things, that is behind all things, from which all things have come and are continually coming'—That spirit is Me.

This body is one of my infinite *adharas*.[6] This *chitta*[7] is one of my infinite adharas. There is a *chitta-loka,* a mind-world. Of this mind-world, I am master. What is called the lower self is a part of the chitta-loka and the body which that particular part has chosen for itself. The infinite can play on the Infinitesimal. I, illimitable, indivisible, omni-potent, can for my *leela* [8] choose this little frame and this little mind. Ay, and put infinite energies and force into the 'little' mind.

I am God, simply God.

I am the Self, the only Self.

5

My nature is Light.

I am the Seer—the Light that sees all and sees that it sees— the pure Knower. Even chitta is unconscious; it reflects my light. But, I am both conscious and unconscious. I am God.

The chitta is a nest of subtle things—sparks or seeds which are placed there as the result of past mental action. The chitta is a whole sea of such things. It is a maze. Now these sparks reflect my light. But they take each other for 'conscious' sparks. The Earth looks at Mars and says, 'Lo, there revolves a shining planet.' And Mars looks at the Earth and says, 'Lo, there wheels an orb of light.' Yet Neither has any intrinsic light of its own. Both reflect the light of the sun. So are these seeds of the mind. The eye and the light are above—they are in me. Thoughts are not conscious motions, they are motions in the presence of the great conscious. I am the light, the light, the Light. I am God.

O, is it true that I have been falsely dreaming—dreaming for long in the past, that I had wants, that I had troubles, that I had cares? Is it true that Indra was for sometime wallowing in the mire in a pig's form? Is it true that Siva the lord was mad for a while? Is it true that Vishnu, the All-pervading, had to pass through several births—as fish, tortoise, pig, half-man, mannikin, and man, before he could manifest himself as a full-blown god-man—ay, God on Earth?[9] Yes, this is all true.

But why? Why should the *atma*[10] forget himself? The atma forgets nought. The atma is self-luminous and so, omniscient. He is all there is. Could He not know all? But Evolution is his leela. Evolution is the play he has chosen. He is infinite at all centres. But He is also finite at all centres. Each centre, knowing itself as finite, goes through the process of evolution. When perfection is reached and it knows itself as infinite, then it is in endless joy, and helps the other centres to follow the Path.

6

Behold! The Divine Stream is flowing into the *prana-sarira* and eats up seeds of Fear.
I am God.
What shall I fear?
And why?
It is for fear of Me, the Upanishad says, that the sun shines, the fire burns, the wind blows and the worlds revolve.

All things fear ME. I am positive to all things. All things are negative to ME. I command, They obey.

What shall I fear?

And why?

'He who knows the joy of the Brahman, he fears nought, he fears never.'

I know the joy of the Brahman.

For I am the Brahman.

7

The *Gunas*.[11] I transcend them. I am *nistraigunya*.[12] I am God. I am God. I am God.

I owe nothing to anybody. How can I be indebted? I am God— the Prime Principle of Good. All the good things that all the creatures possess are my gifts—given out of my Love.

I gave Rockefeller his wealth. I gave Wilhelm his empire, I gave Togo his fame, I gave Ramamurti his strength. All, all that princes, poets, artists, generals and the rest of men possess, are my gifts, given out of my love. I am the giver, I receive not. I give all that men want; they have but to come and ask and lo! I give like the *kalpa-taru*.[13]

I owe nothing to anyone. Debts have I none. The Universe is mine; it is indebted to me for its very existence.

I give, I give, I give.

8

All powers are mine.

By my Will, the suns move and the planets revolve around them.

By my Will, the infinite systems are moving and vibrating in infinite space, and the infinite existences do exist.

I am God—all-Powerful—*Sarva Saktiman*. All the tendencies, all the knowings and all the actions of the Universe are mine.

I am the Lord, the Spirit, the Life and the Being of the Universe.

I care not for powers, for they are mine already. I care not for finite things, as the Infinite is mine. All that this particular adhara, that I have chosen in a particular centre for my leela, requires, shall come unto it, unheedful and unasked-for.

I shall make no demands, I shall merely expect all good things for this adhara. Ay, ay, I love this body, else how could I have chosen it for my manifestation?

But I love it as my vehicle, as my servant, as the animal that is here to be used by Me, but not as the Self, never.

This body and this mind, which I use as tools, shall get all things that are good for them.

This mind of mine is My temple.

I shall keep it clean, pure, wholesome, strong and beautiful.

It is my golden shrine.

And My heart is the Holy of Holies.

Being filled with Me—the *Atman*—this body and this mind shall convey all my glorious powers to the rest of the world for the amelioration, upheaval and protection of the latter.

My organs shall be vehicles of the Divine Force, which flowing shall reach out the corners of the world and help invigorate, purify and elevate all that may be found on its way. I am God—the Omnipotent.

My blessings go forth to the world.

Behold, I bless all, all of whatever race or nation. Even those nations of the barbarous realms, whom men count as cruel, greedy, and godless, even them I bless.

For they are all Myself.

I ordain that all these men shall have the brute in them slain and the god in them liberated.

I ordain that all these men grow more and more godly, high-minded and tolerant.

I ordain that all hate and hypocrisy, all desire for godless power and ill-gotten gold, shall disappear among the races of men.

Ay, disappear if not by peace, then by suffering,

For nothing shall stand against the Will of God.

Great and unnameable shall be the suffering of those who resist the Will of God.

I ordain that there shall be equality, mutual tolerance and regard among the children of men.

I bless all, I want all men to be happy and joyous. I want that there should be no disease or famine or war among the races of men.

I bless all, I want that there should be no jails and no hospitals, and no need for them. May mankind have happiness, peace, and plenty. May they grow in Wisdom and in true Power.

May they make the path of evolution towards God easy and painless, both for themselves and the lower animals.

May all creatures feel My joy—the joy of the pure Atman.

May all sentient beings be filled with love and godly power.

May Love be the ruler of this Universe.

Good, Good be to all, all, all.

9

I have no agitations, mental unrests.

I am the Great Equilibrium.

I am Peace, Peace, Peace.

Nothing can move me.

Nothing can upset me, nothing can jar on me.

Nothing can ruffle my temper.

I am nistraigunya—beyond the three gunas. I am Peace, Peace, Peace.

I am the Lord Vishnu, resting on the Primal Serpent of Wisdom, afloat on the sea of milk—the sea of the milk of pure, spotless, cool, radiant peace.

I am Vishnu. I am Narayana, I am the *Parandhama*, the *Sarvesvara, Sarva-Santi-maya.*

10

The truth is I am one with, hence I am, the Supreme Being. But still I am conscious of a personality which I very often consider to be myself and which, although it is part of the All, still can conceive of itself as a separate, finite entity and act in accordance with that conception.

Anything which considers itself as a separate small entity in this illimitable Universe, illimitable in all ways natural, tends to have interests peculiar to itself as a part from the whole and tends, therefore, to put itself in opposition to the whole in a few respects. The result is what we call pain. What you think, that you are. When you take yourself as but an infinitesimal particle of consciousness, set adrift helpless, in this frightfully immense world, you become so. The result is: you fear, and with reason. For how can a particle be safe, secure and happy (and it wants to be all this) when it is surrounded by an Infinity which is at best indifferent to its little self?

There is no safety, no permanent gratification for what takes itself to be a cell in an ocean.

When men cannot realize themselves as the *Paramatman,* the Supreme Being, the next best thing for them to do is to take themselves as parts of a whole with which they are in perfect harmony and accord.

When you cannot know yourself as the Being of the Universe, try at least to make peace with the Universe, Peace entire and unconditional.

Notes

Brief Chronology of Life and Publications

1. See e.g. S. Muthiah, 'The first Tamil newspapers', 25 Sept. 2017, The *Hindu*, available at https://www.thehindu.com/society/first-newspapers-of-tamil-nadu/article19751056.ece (last visited 17 Jan. 2021).

Introduction

1. The Asian koel is a type of cuckoo, *Eudynamys scolopaceus,* renowned in the Indian cultural tradition for its song.
2. Draupadi, wife to the five Pandava brothers, was a famous example of polyandry, a social system that continues to exist in parts of South Asia (and elsewhere).
3. Michael Wood, *The Story of India,* episode 1 See https:// www. pbs.org/thestoryofindia/ (last visited 1 Mar. 2021).
4. It is worth noting that the Madras government also paid a small sum to Chellamma and each of Bharati's two daughters when they purchased the works from Viswanatha Iyer: see Mira T. Sundara Rajan, 'Moral Rights in the Public Domain: Copyright Matters in

the Works of Indian National Poet C. Subramania Bharati', 2001
Sing. J. Leg. Stud. 161 (2001) at 166.

5. She wrote: 'Vande Mataram—People of the Tamil country! . . .
I will undertake the responsibility of publishing all of Bharati's
works in my lifetime, and afterwards, I have decided to
bequeath them to the people of Tamil Nadu.' Chellamma
Bharati, Preface to the First Volume of Bharati's Complete
Works, entitled *National Songs* (1922), translated by S. Vijaya
Bharati.

6. S. Vijaya Bharati, ed., *Standard Edition: Mahakavi Bharatiyar
Kavithaigal,* Volumes 1–4 (*Desiya Githangal; Deivam
Thatthuvam; Kannan Pattu, Panchali Sabatham, Kuyil Pattu;* and
Bharati Vazhkkaiyum Pira Padalkal) (Vijaya Bharati Publishing
via CreateSpace Independent Publishing Platform, 2015).

7. Furthering her experiments with technology on behalf of Bharati,
Vijaya Bharati also created a blog dedicated to the poet. Her novel
goal was to publish widely about the poet in the English language,
thereby reaching Bharati's fellow Indians and fellow citizens of
the world who are not necessarily fluent in Tamil: see https://
subramaniabharati.com.

8. See *Agni and Other Poems and Translations & Essays and Other
Prose Fragments,* by C. Subrahmanya [sic] Bharati, Natarajan
Publishers, Chennai, 1980. It contains a Foreword by C.R.
Reddy and K.S. Venkatamani, and a Publishers' Note stating:
'We are very much indebted to Sri. C. Visvanatha Ayyar, [half-]
brother of the poet and editor of the first edition, for not only
agreeing to edit this edition also, but also supplying us with
the additional matter included in this volume and for his other
valuable suggestions.' The editors also note the first publication
date of Bharati's English writings by Bharati Prachuralayam
as 1937.

9. Ibid. This book, now out of print, was, for a long time, the only
available collection of Bharati's writing in English after the 1937

publication. Despite the excellent intentions of the Editors, the book contains many printing errors and also includes works of doubtful authenticity.

10. In her celebrated work *A Room of One's Own* (1929), Woolf writes: 'the androgynous mind is resonant and porous; . . . it transmits emotion without impediment; . . . it is naturally creative, incandescent and undivided. In fact one goes back to Shakespeare's mind as the type of the androgynous, of the man-womanly mind, though it would be impossible to say what Shakespeare thought of women. And if it be true that it is one of the tokens of the fully developed mind that it does not think specially or separately of sex, how much harder it is to attain that condition now than ever before.' Virginia Woolf, *A Room of One's Own* (Mariner Books, New York, 1989; first published 1929), p. 98.

11. Also one of the twelve Alwars, Tamil saints focusing on the worship of Vishnu. Andal, too, lived during the eighth century.

12. All of the English translations of his poems published here correspond directly to Bharati's Tamil originals, and the title of the Tamil poem is given with the translation. The previous publication of Bharati's English works in 1980 included a small number of poems in English for which no Tamil original by Bharati exists. These 'translations' are invariably rendered in an English style that reads completely unlike Bharati's own. We believe that they are clear instances of misattribution, a problem that has also proven to be endemic to the publication of Bharati's Tamil works. Accordingly, they have been deliberately excluded from the present collection.

13. In fact, Tagore's English translation of his Bengali original, *Gitanjali,* was admired by W.B. Yeats and secured Tagore the Nobel Prize in Literature in1913. It remains the only Nobel Prize ever awarded to an Indian writer. However, Yeats and others later criticized Tagore's work; see Amartya Sen, 'Tagore and his

India', first published 28 Aug. 2001, Nobel Media AB 2021, available at https://www.nobelprize.org/prizes/literature/1913/ tagore/article/ (footnote omitted) (last visited 28 Jan. 2021). Tagore himself is said to have remained unsatisfied with English translations of his poetry, including his own, throughout his life.

14. Ibid.
15. A notable exception is the remarkable work of Professor Vidya Dehejia: see e.g. 'Poetic Visions of the Great Goddess: Tamil Nadu', in *Devi, The Great Goddess: Female Divinity in South Asian Art,* exh. cat., Smithsonian Institution, Washington, D.C., 1999, p. 10. A well-known translation of Bharati's poem 'Wind' is also widely attributed to A.K. Ramanujan, a modern Indian poet and scholar.
16. Quoted in Sen, note 14 above.
17. John Keats' ambition was to be 'among the English poets': quoted in *Essential Keats,* Selected and with an Introduction by Philip Levine, *The Essential Poets Series* (HarperCollins, New York 1987), xxii–xxiii.

Part I: The National Movement

Chapter 1: The Political Evolution in the Madras Presidency

This detailed article sets the scene for Bharati's life and activities in south India, and it provides important background information on the development of the national movement in this part of the country. The story told here reveals the troubling interplay of British and French interests and sensibilities around the tiny yet strategically significant territory of Pondicherry (now known as Puducherry). The ruthlessness of all parties concerned is only occasionally punctuated by the resurgence of human values (notably, on the part of 'certain French magistrates'). This history is little known today, but it is a part of India's national struggle and of twentieth-century world history that craves to be remembered. Bharati describes the conditions of perpetual uncertainty and, indeed, persecution in which the nationalists exiled to Pondicherry lived—foremost among them, of course, Bharati himself.

1. C.I.D. stood for the 'Criminal Investigation Department' of the British Police.

2. The case is also discussed by Bharati in his 'Police Rule in India' (see below and accompanying text).

3. As stated by the Madras High Court, the reduced sentence was to be '6 (six) years' transportation': see In Re: V.O. Chidambaram Pillai vs Unknown on 4 November 1908, 1 Ind Cas 36, available at https://indiankanoon.org/doc/149350/; and In Re: Subramania Siva vs Unknown on 4 November 1908, 1 Ind Cas 22, available at https://indiankanoon.org/doc/657853/ (last visited 1 Nov. 2020). 'Transportation' has been defined by the Constitution Bench of the Indian Supreme Court as 'a sentence of rigorous imprisonment in jails in India': see e.g. Balwant Singh Malik, 'The Law of Punishments of Transportation for Life and Imprisonment for Life—A Critical Appraisal' (1999) 5 SCC (Jour) 4 [citing *Gopal Vinayak Godse* v. *State of Maharashtra*, (1961) 3 SCR 440], available at http://www.ebc- india.com/lawyer/articles/9905a2.htm#:~:text=%22Before%20Act%2026%20of%201955,imprisonment%20for%20the%20same%20term (last visited 1 Nov. 2020).

4. The *Entente Cordiale* of 8 April 1904, was, as summarized by the Encyclopedia Britannica, the 'Anglo-French agreement that, by settling a number of controversial matters, ended antagonisms between Great Britain and France and paved the way for their diplomatic cooperation against German pressures in the decade

preceding World War I (1914–18)': https://www.britannica.
com/event/Entente-Cordiale (last visited 22 Jan. 2021).

5. Bharati's point about the 'sentimental' (i.e. symbolic) significance
of Pondicherry is well made: Joseph-François Dupleix was first
member of the superior council of Pondicherry and then governor-
general of French India. Dupleix made several failed attempts
to expand French influence in India. See the Britannica entries
on Dupleix (https://www.britannica.com/biography/Joseph-
Francois-Dupleix) and Puducherry (https://www.britannica.
com/place/Puducherry-union-territory-India#ref487139) (last
visited 22 Jan. 2021).

6. Mahe, located on the Western Malabar coast, surrounded by
what is now Kerala, was one of four French colonies in India.
Encyclopedia Britannica has an entry on Mahe, https://www.
britannica.com/place/Mahe-India, as well as a useful map of
French India in the entry on Puducherry (https://www.britannica.
com/place/Puducherry-union-territory-India#ref487139) (last
visited 22 Jan. 2021).

7. One hundred thousand rupees; enormous funds then, this would
amount to about $1300 at today's exchange rate.

Chapter 2: India and the World

Bharati's anxieties about India were many: not only was he concerned
about the state of the country under British rule, but he was also
preoccupied by the larger question of India's stature in the eyes of
the world. Accordingly, India's participation in the War, in Bharati's
eyes, could not be anything but open-hearted and open-handed. He
urges Indians to adopt the moral high ground, arguing, as always, for a
'lov[ing]' approach even to the colonialists, pointing out that 'deeds will
count before the gods' even where 'men' may fail to recognize them.

Bharati was anxious that England should understand India's
'beautiful message', and that 'the utter nobility and love' underlying

India's willingness to fight in Britain's aid should be appreciated. Above all, England and the world should recognize India's approach as 'foreshadowing . . . a higher human civilization'. That new civilization would be one where enslavement through empire, and the relationship of domination and subjugation between countries and between people, would be forgotten. Bharati foresaw the impending reality of a post-colonial world and he was anxious to formulate the ideals suited to it—though the world has yet to live up to his expectations.

1. The Sikhs and the Rajputs are both groups traditionally renowned for their military prowess. The Sikhs came to be known as the 'Lions of the Great War'. See e.g. Arjun Singh Flora, 'Lions of the Great War', 22 Aug. 2009, available at https://www.firstworldwar.com/features/lionsofthegreatwar.htm (last visited 23 Feb. 2021).

2. Dr Jagdish Chandra Bose (1858–1937), a Bengali scientist whose extraordinary range of activities makes it difficult to classify him within a single discipline: see Chapter 26, 'To the Being of the Universe', below.

3. Usually, 'Machiavellianism'; the term is defined by the Oxford English Dictionary as 'cunning, scheming, and unscrupulous, especially in politics' (https://www.lexico.com/definition/machiavellian). It is derived from the name of Niccolò Machiavelli, an Italian statesman and author of *The Prince* (1532), which espoused these methods.

Chapter 3: India and the War

In this essay and the following letter, 'Home and War', Bharati expresses his deep concern that the intervention of World War I would cause the British to postpone needed reforms in India and, above all, that Indian nationalist priorities would be sidelined by Britain. Bharati outlines India's extraordinary contribution to the War effort, which included the commitment of troops and other sacrifices, and argues that India's support grew out of moral conviction, including her specific belief that the Allies were fighting for a more just world order in the wake of the War. However, in Bharati's view, India had received scant recognition for her support of Britain in the War. He hoped to educate the British about the pressing goals of Indians, namely, education, police reform, and the promotion of Indian industry. He considers this the essential business of everyday life and argues that the urgency of wartime should, in no respect, override these needs.

As usual, Bharati adopts a high moral tone in this essay towards India's colonizers—as if, by doing so, he expected them to act according to the moral imperatives that seem obvious to him. 'England will never forget India's generosity and magnanimity,' he writes; once the War is over, England would remember India's sacrifices and reward her with the independence that she sought. It is worth remembering that British rule of the latter part of the nineteenth century was characterized by a struggle to justify the British presence in India on moral grounds, so Bharati's appeals resonate with the times—though the view from the twenty-first century is necessarily more sceptical.

It is truly a pity that Bharati had to plead with the British government to 'Give us light!' In his Tamil poem, 'Bharata Nadu', Bharati takes just the opposite stance, describing India's glory, her resources, her achievements, her qualities, and her spirituality. In his eyes, India was a 'giver of light' to the world.

1. For Bharati's exploration of the Nietzchean ideal of the 'superman', see his essay on the subject: 'The Siddha and the Superman'.

2. Bharati is no doubt referring to Rudyard Kipling here, who famously wrote that 'East is East and West is West, and never the twain shall meet.' Kipling (1865–1936) received the Nobel Prize for literature in 1907, but his modern reputation, in the West as in

India, is controversial. Kipling's position, as expressed in this 'Ballad of East and West', could never have found favour with Bharati.

Chapter 5: Mr Tilak and the British Government

Bal Gangadhar Tilak (1856–1920) was the national leader of the Extremist faction of the Congress party. Bharati considered Tilak his political *guru*. Bharati had the opportunity to meet with the leaders of both the Extremist and the Moderate parties at the Surat Congress in December of 1907, which was attended by Tilak, Lajpat Roy, Aurobindo Ghose, and Gokhale, among others. S. Vijaya Bharati describes the impression that Tilak made on Bharati: 'Bharati was greatly impressed by Tilak's majestic appearance—his turban, which was entwined in circles around his head; his moustache, which seemed to challenge the British Empire; his strong face which showed unwavering determination; his eyes, expressive of love and the breadth of his wisdom. His voice and eloquence, and his perseverance towards attaining his goal, fascinated Bharati. He became an ardent disciple of Tilak, and believed deeply in Tilak's political principles and methods.'

Bharati wrote two poems in Tamil on Tilak, '*Lokamanya Balaganghadara Tilakar*' (Lokamanya, meaning Leader of the People, was Tilak's honorary title); and '*Vazhga Tilakan Namam*'. He calls him the *tilakam* (ornament) on the forehead of Bharata Devi (the divine goddess India, as Bharati envisioned her); he writes that the name Tilak is chanted by Indian patriots as Saivite devotees chant the name of Lord Siva.

Chapter 6: In Thine Arms Again

Bharati's poem was inspired by the tribulations of Indian freedom-fighters who were imprisoned by the British. Notably, in 1907, Tilak was sentenced on a charge of sedition and was imprisoned for six years in the Mandalay jail; he was released in June 1914, at the onset of

World War I. Lajpat Roy, a member of the Indian Congress, was also deported to Burma in 1907. Bharati wrote two poems on this latter occasion, 'Salutation to Lajpat Roy' and 'The Lamentation of Lajpat Roy'. 'In Thine Arms Again' celebrates the return of India's chosen leaders to their Motherland; the Mother bestows her blessings and gifts of happiness upon them.

Chapter 7: In Memoriam

Bharati had met Gokhale (1866–1915), the leader of the Moderate Party, at the Surat Congress, a great gathering of nationalists in the closing days of 1907. He respected Gokhale's principles and his dedication to his country, but he did not share Gokhale's views of progress in India.

Gokhale had been invited by the British government to India House, to discuss possible reforms with a view to improving India's situation. Gokhale hoped that the British Government would take his ideas and suggestions seriously, and act upon them.

In his satirical poem on Gokhale, 'The Song of the Gokhale Sanyasin', Bharati talks about the Moderate Party's satisfaction in the attempts of Lord Morley, Secretary of State, to bring reforms into effect; he challenges Gokhale's hope that reforms will eventually happen, 'one of these days'. In Bharati's opinion, the promised reforms were simply false. They were never going to happen.

As Bharati remarks in this article: 'Even today there must be certain political thinkers in our country who may not approve of Gokhale's life in everything that he did or could not do.' Bharati's political methods differed from Gokhale's; yet he could not fail to appreciate Gokhale's dedication to his country, and the sacrifices he made for the betterment of India. He considered him a true nationalist and a humanitarian, and this is clear in his concluding words: '[M]ay his soul rest in peace. His country has accepted his Dharma.'

In another poem, 'The Moderates Find Fault with Patriotism', Bharati describes how the Moderates blame the Extremists—and, in particular, Tilak, their leader—for actions which, in their view, caused the situation in the country to deteriorate. He is ultimately contemptuous of the Moderates' complaints about the Extremists—complaints made, absurdly enough, to the British Government.

Chapter 8: The Fox with the Golden Tail

This acerbic satire is directed at Annie Besant, a British social reformer who ultimately became an important figure in the Indian Independence movement, and who was both admired and criticized by Bharati. In 1907, Besant became the president of the Theosophical Society. This spiritual organization was founded by Helena Blavatsky and Henry Steel Olcutt in New York City, in 1875, and eventually established its International Headquarters in the Madras suburb of Adyar. In 1909, the fourteen-year old J. Krishnamurti was 'discovered' and declared to be the 'World Teacher' that the Theosophists had been awaiting. Krishnamurti and his brother, Nityananda, were placed under the care of the Theosophists. With the initial consent of the boys' father, Annie Besant became the legal guardian of the boys. The relationship between Krishnamurti and Besant grew to be close, and he considered her his surrogate mother.

In his Preface to the Second Edition of 'The Fox with the Golden Tail', Bharati explains the 'esoteric meaning' of his fable. In the long history of India, while 'the ancient Hindus had scaled the extreme heights of spiritual realization,' the English-educated men of more recent times were 'the biggest gulls of any age or country.' This was one of the consequences of India's enslavement under foreign rule. Indians not only suffered for the satisfaction of their basic needs, but they had also become psychologically dependent on the British. In this context, Indians were subjected to 'the most colossal spiritual fraud of the ages.'

Notwithstanding Bharati's ironic tone in this article, he deeply respected Besant's national activities in support of women's freedom and democracy in India. Bharati wrote several articles in *New India* and *Commonweal,* publications led by Annie Besant, in the years 1914–15.

1.   This Second Edition of 'The Fox with the Golden Tail' was published as a small booklet and was printed at Saigon Sinnaya Press, Pondicherry.

Chapter 9: Reflections

Bharati immensely admired Rabindranath Tagore (1861–1941), considered the greatest of modern Bengali poets. Yet the contrast between the two men could not be more striking. Tagore was born into wealth and privilege. He toured the world, and one of the direct consequences of his international opportunities for exposure was the award of the Nobel Prize in literature for his work. Tagore received the Nobel in 1913, upon the appearance of his poetic collection *Gitanjali* in Europe, in English translation. A foreword was provided by no less a literary personality than William Butler Yeats, who would himself become a recipient of the Nobel Prize in 1923. Tagore was subsequently awarded a knighthood by the British monarch, in 1915, only to return it, in protest against the Jallianwala Bagh massacre, in 1919.

Tagore was, of course, a supporter of Indian independence, though his views on nationalism were complicated; and, at least on this terrain, the two poets could meet as literary and spiritual brothers. For Bharati, Tagore's international achievements were inspiring, and his readiness to celebrate them, in spite of his own unrealized ambitions to travel the world, shows the greatness of his character. Indeed, in these 'Reflections' on the issue of national pride, he exhorts the public to embrace the achievements of their fellow-Indians when they prove to be outstanding, and to be inspired by them to reach for greatness in their own turn. This attitude, he feels, will promote a 'contagion of greatness' in the country. His writing is informed by his deep conviction that individual freedom implies, above all, the potential for remarkable acts. 'Go watch thyself or watch thy brother,' he writes, in typical style; 'either of you will soon be great.'

He goes a step further: the way to greatness, he writes, is revealed by the sacred writings of India and, in particular, the ideal of *karma-yoga* described in the *Bhagavad Gita*. He explains this as dedication to one's work in a 'spirit of self-surrender'. The lesson that he emphasizes from the well-known discourse on the nature of work in the *Bhagavad Gita* is the value inherent in each person's deeds, whatever may be the respective field of endeavour (or, indeed, the person's social standing). Means count as much as ends. Built into this perspective is an inherent morality since, under such a philosophical system, supposedly great ends can never be justified by immoral means. In this, too, Bharati shows the uniqueness of the Indian cultural perspective that he advances. It also presents an interesting comparison with the modern West.

Narrating the great deeds of outstanding Indians, he writes, is the glorious duty of India's 'great journalists' and 'great publicists'. He was one among their number, working as a journalist throughout his life, dedicated to the nationalist cause.

1. Rabindranth Tagore (1861–1941), famed Bengali writer and nationalist, whose *Gitanjali* won him the friendship of Yeats, and, in 1913, the Nobel Prize. Bharati translated a few of Tagore's short stories into Tamil and greatly respected the Bengali poet's achievements.

2. Swami Vivekananda (1863–1902) founded the Ramakrishna Math order of monks in honor of his guru, Ramakrishna. He played a leading role in introducing Indian philosophy to the West. Sister Nivedita, Bharati's own guru, was a devotee of Swami Vivekananda; see note on Chapter 17, 'New Birth', below.

3.   *Karma-yoga,* as described here by Bharati, is the *yoga,* or path to
     God, made possible by devotion to one's work *(Bhagavad Gita).*

Chapter 11: Patriotism and Religious Differences

The Indian National Congress was initially a political party that
ultimately developed into a vehicle for the Indian Independence
Movement. The Indian Congress was split into two parties, the
'Extremists' and the 'Moderates'. Great leaders were to be found on
both sides. The Moderates included Dadabai Naoroji, Gopal Krishna
Gokhale, and Firoz Shah Mehta, while the Extremists counted
among their ranks Lajpat Roy, Bal Gangadhar Tilak, Bipin Chandra
Pal, and Sri Aurobindo. In the South, V. Krishnaswamy Iyer was the
leader of the Moderates, while Bharati, V.O. Chidambaram Pillai,
Subramania Siva, G. Subramania Iyer, and Surendranath Arya were
Extremists.

Bharati's writing on religious differences among the nationalists
shows the sophistication of his views: the goals of privacy, secularism,
and diversity are paramount in his mind. On this last point, the
importance that he ascribes to diversity *for its own sake* is noteworthy,
pointing out that homogeneity of religious or spiritual views—
'conformity'—is, quite simply, 'dangerous'. With this approach, he
sees no reason why Indians from all backgrounds should not work
together towards the establishment of a free nation. As usual in
Bharati's case, his perspectives were not only relevant to the Indian
nationalism of his day, but also to its modern incarnation—and to the
broader struggles of democracy worldwide in the twenty-first century.

1.   Shudras are traditionally the fourth of the four castes in India's
     caste system, finding themselves at the bottom of the hierarchy in
     which Brahmanas, or Brahmins, are at the top. Needless to say,
     Bharati deplored this system; see, for example, Chapter 21, 'The
     Crime of Caste', below.

2.   Brahmin males traditionally wore their hair in a 'tuft', while the tradition of marking the forehead with various special substances—sandalwood, ash, turmeric, or saffron powder, for example—is common to many Hindu groups.

3.   The sacred thread is another Brahmin tradition: conferred upon Brahmin boys as they reach adulthood, they are supposed never to remove it. Among other things, it represents the right to be initiated into the study of the Sanskrit scriptures. In a well-known incident, Bharati performed a sacred thread ceremony for one of his non-Brahmin disciples, Kanagalingam, who subsequently wrote about the event.

Chapter 12: Free Speech

Bharati suffered enormously under British censorship. His own magazines were shut down, and his writings proscribed, effectively leaving him without any means of livelihood. This was the fundamental reason behind the poet's material 'poverty', which, as should be obvious to his readers, was by no means his choice or desire. Bharati was compelled to seek shelter in French-controlled Pondicherry, where he spent more than a decade in exile. His experiences there are elucidated in the first essay in this volume, 'The Political Evolution in the Madras Presidency', which paints a deeply disturbing picture of continuing British oppression, with the partial collaboration of the French, against nationalist exiles in the territory.

In this short essay on free speech, Bharati draws attention to the hypocrisy of the colonialists, who are proud of free speech as one of the institutions of British democracy but reserve the enjoyment of this basic human right to themselves. If the English truly believe in free speech, Bharati points out, then they are under the imperative to recognize Indians' right to it, too. Once again, Bharati's demand for equality was ahead of its time. It remains only partially realized in the post-colonial world order, where injustice continues to find its place despite a rhetoric of international equality among nations and peoples.

Chapters 13 & 14: Rights and Duties

This subject understandably preoccupied Bharati. The appeal to broader principles of reason and humanity was a key element in his struggle against the British—ideas that British writers and thinkers had, themselves, long espoused but (conveniently) failed to apply to India and Indians. In his comments here, the reader can sense the poet's impatience with an abstract approach to philosophical doctrines. In this case, the rather speculative philosophical exercise leads to conclusions that are 'misleading', ultimately trivializing the notion of 'rights', in particular—a concept of enormous practical, as well as moral, significance.

Bharati's writings in English aim to show that the imperialist position was unjustifiable based on the very ideas and values that the British held most dear. Free speech was one; the concept of rights, as illustrated by these brief yet illuminating notes, was another. Bharati's understanding of rights and the social role that they play is as sophisticated as any lawyer's, yet his explanation of the concept could hardly be simpler. Rights allow society to proceed on some basis other than that referred to elsewhere by Bharati as the 'stupid doctrine that "Might is Right"'. They are the conception that holds society in balance, protecting the vulnerable from exploitation while restraining the powerful, and thereby providing the basis for a society governed by law rather than the arbitrary exercise of power.

It should be noted that Bharati was especially well placed to discuss rights and duties in the context of interpreting the *Bhagavad Gita*. He was learned in the Sanskrit language, even writing Sanskrit poetry (notably, his devotional song *Booloka Kumari,* 'Queen of the World'). Bharati not only studied the *Gita* and other Sanskrit texts, but he also crafted his own translation of the *Gita* in Tamil.

1. The expression commonly used today would probably be 'abuse of power'.

Chapter 15: Police Rule in India

This 'letter' was originally published as an open letter in *The Hindu* of 10 February 1914, under the heading, 'Police Rule in India'. By writing to this key leader of an opposition party, and one who stood for social democratic ideals that would have appealed to Bharati, the poet no doubt hoped to stir up public sentiment in Britain in his favour. Indeed, Bharati had maintained his anti-imperial stance with the meticulous precision of a lawyer, demonstrating, patiently and systematically, the flaws in British reasoning, the irrationality of the charges against himself and other nationalist figures, and the hypocrisy in Britain's espousal of ideals such as free speech and civil rights when these were categorically denied to Indians. Had he managed to find an audience in the halls of British political life, who knows what the effects might have been? Exposure of British behaviour in India may have hurt the government while improving conditions of life for the nationalists. Given the history of his powerful and unwavering defences against British charges, we can be sure that Bharati had given careful thought to all of these implications and pursued a conscious strategy on this and almost every other occasion.

It is a disturbing letter. The treatment of the nationalists in south India is a bitter lesson in the cruelty of imperial rule. It is a story that has not yet been told in full to the world. It must ultimately emerge as part of history's broader reckoning with hatred and bigotry.

1. Ramsay MacDonald (1866–1937) was the leader of the British Labour Party from 1911 to 1914, resigning at that point due to his opposition to Britain's engagement in World War I; in 1924, he became the first Labour prime minister of Britain. His biography is available at the Encyclopedia Britannica website,

https://www.britannica.com/biography/Ramsay-MacDonald, and on the BBC History website: http://www.bbc.co.uk/ history/historic_figures/macdonald_ramsay.shtml (last visited 5 Aug. 2020).

2. This section of the Indian Penal Code deals with sedition; it continues to be present in the modern code and is a highly controversial aspect of Indian law: see https://indiankanoon.org/doc/1641007/.

3. *Quod erat demonstrandum* (which was to be demonstrated). The end of a formal proof, also used to signify that one's claim has been proven—here, of course, it is Bharati's sarcastic reference to the illogical and irrational nature of the charges.

4. Paul Bluysen (1861–1929), French journalist and politician; the history of his political service is summarized on the website of the French National Assembly, http://www2.assemblee-nationale.fr/ sycomore/fiche/(num_dept)/882 (last visited 1 Nov. 2020).

5. Judge of inquiry: in the French legal system, the 'magistrate responsible for conducting the investigative hearing that precedes a criminal trial. In this hearing the major evidence is gathered and presented, and witnesses are heard and depositions taken. If the juge d'instruction is not convinced that there is sufficient evidence of guilt to warrant a trial at the end of the proceedings, no trial will occur.' See Encyclopedia Britannica online, available at https://www.britannica.com/topic/juge-dinstruction (last visited 1 Nov. 2020).

6. The Tinnevely Riot occurred on 17 March 1908, in response to the conviction of Indian Nationalists Subramania Siva and V.O. Chidambaram Pillai by Judge Pinhey, also referenced by Bharati in his article on 'The Political Evolution in the Madras Presidency', (Chapter 1, above) on charges of sedition under the Indian Penal Code. The incident is discussed by Mohammed Imranullah S., "Remembering 7 July 1908, the judgement day," *The Hindu*, 7 July 2014, available at https://www.thehindu.com/ news/cities/Madurai/remembering-july-7-1908-the-judgement-

day/article6185099.ece (last visited 1 Nov. 2020); the appellate judgement is available at file:///Users/mira/Downloads/b'In_Re__Subramania_Siva_vs_Unknown_on_4_November,_1908'. PDF (last visited 1 Nov. 2020). Chidambaram Pillai became famous as '*Kapalottiya Tamizhan*' (the 'Tamilian who Steered a Ship'), the man who launched the first local shipping company to compete with the British shipping monopoly of the times, in particular, between Tuticorin (now Thoothukudi, south India) and Colombo (Sri Lanka). Bharati and V.O.C. were 'close' friends: see S. Vijaya Bharati, *C. Subramania Bharati* (Publications Divison, Ministry of Information and Broadcasting, Government of India, 1972) at 42–43.

Chapter 16: The Coming Age

Bharati's goal was to re-establish *Krita-yuga*, the epoch of human enlightenment, peace, and prosperity, in the modern world. Yet, in this short essay, the poet shows himself to be simultaneously an idealist and a keen and cynical observer of human nature—or, at least, human behaviour. If 'perfect fellowship' cannot be attained then, at least, let us aspire to 'mutual harmlessness'. 'Even legislators,' he writes, feel a moral compulsion to 'pretend to work' towards this goal, so fundamental is it to human society! His expectations of political actors were tempered with realism and, indeed, shrewdness.

Bharati was not alone in his belief that competition is the root of all evil. He views competition for both 'necessities' and 'luxuries' as being equally detrimental to human society. His solution, common ownership of 'land and water' seems more remote than ever before. Nevertheless, the growing climate crisis shows the continued relevance and, indeed, urgency of implementing social models that, in contrast to modern capitalism, do not encourage the exploitation of resources by wealthy owners at the expense of the population at large.

Like other thinkers of his time, as is apparent in this article, it is fair to say that Bharati sympathized with truly socialist ways of seeing the world—socialist in the sense of an ideal philosophical perspective, and not a political system. It would be an exaggeration to call him an exponent of socialist theory in the Western sense of the term; Bharati himself points out that Western socialist thought had gained little exposure in India at that time.

Interestingly, Bharati was a great supporter of the Russian Revolution, which he learned about as a journalist when it first occurred. Bharati's poem on the Russian Revolution, entitled 'Puthiya Russia' (*The New Russia*), is a celebration of the birth of a new democracy, and compares the fall of the Tsar to 'the fall of the Himalayas'. To Bharati, and to many of his contemporaries, the Revolution was a sign that a new and more humanistic way of life was beginning in Russia; they did not foresee that the removal of the Tsar would pave the way for a new system of repression. It was one of the sobering instances when history would prove these contemporary optimists mistaken.

We are left with the proliferation of the social evils identified by Bharati and fewer solutions than ever before.

Chapter 17: New Birth

In this article, Bharati describes his vision of India as Bharata-Shakti, an embodiment of the goddess Parashakti. He writes that he received this vision through Sister Nivedita, a disciple of Swami Vivekananda.

This story, in itself, is unique and wondrous. Sister Nivedita was an Irishwoman, born Margaret Elizabeth Noble, who went to India to help Swami Vivekananda with his plans to improve women's education. Bharati dedicated the first publication of his 'National Songs' to her and considered her his '*guru*'.

Bharati's vision of Bharata-Shakti is unique: she is the life, the soul, of India, the land of Bharata. In his poem 'Our Mother' (*Engal*

Thai), he describes Bharata-Shakti as follows (the population of India was then about three hundred million people, or thirty crores):

> This Shakti has thirty crores of faces and sixty crores of hands, but her soul is one. She speaks eighteen languages, but her thoughts are one. She is the symbol of our culture: our poetry, our music, our paintings, our sculptures – our soil, our rivers, our mountains, our trees – are all Her body; our fame, our valour, our strength, our love, our intellectual pursuits – all are Bharata-Shakti.

Bharati was saddened by the demeaning of the people of India under British rule and he was eager to revive the greatness of India's past. In this article, he rejoices in the birth of the new nation and her impending recognition by the world. The new India that he envisioned was to be all that she had been, and even more. He felt that India's social ills were clouding the radiance of Bharata-Shakti—the evils of caste and superstition, the enslavement of women, the widespread lack of education and freedom. Fear, hunger, and poverty all played a role in casting her down. Bharati further expresses these ideas and emotions in a Tamil poem on 'The Present India and the Future India', where he passionately seeks to drive away the 'present' India with his words and welcomes a 'new' India in her stead.

Part II: Social Justice

Chapter 18, 19 & 20: Bharati on Women

Bharati is recognized as a great proponent of women's rights, and these three articles show just how spectacular his thinking on women's freedom actually was. For his perspective is exactly this: not only are women 'equal' to men, but they are, in his view, spiritually superior. They play a crucial role in propagating civilization, infinitely beyond that of replenishing human population alone. We are unlikely to find another thinker of this period, in India or anywhere else in the world, whose ideas were more advanced than Bharati's in this regard.

In this article and the following two, 'Women's Freedom' and 'Matri-Puja', Bharati discusses the question of women's social status from historical, philosophical, and religious points of view. His goal, with typical insight, is to change *men*—so that they can understand the true nature of women, correct their own attitudes, and act in accordance with what Bharati considered a truly civilized manner. As a social reformer, Bharati believed that his first duty was to educate men, while creating an environment in which women could be educated; the establishment of social equality between the sexes was his goal.

Two remarks should be made about Bharati's feminism. First, like many other Indian nationalists, Bharati closely identified womanhood with India; women were a symbol of the country. Because he was a poet and a visionary, that symbolism took on forms that were particularly dramatic, compelling, rich, and complex in his poetry and other writings. For Bharati, India's freedom and the freedom of Indian women were one and the same goal. By uplifting women, freedom for India would simultaneously be achieved.

In a celebrated Tamil poem, Bharati describes a 'New Kind of Woman' ('*Pudumai Penn*'), who would be equal to man in all respects, intellectually and otherwise, a lawmaker for the new and liberated country, and a personality capable of realizing the ultimate goal of freedom for India.

Interestingly, Bharati's radical awakening to women's rights can be traced to a specific incident, recounted by Chellamma Bharati in her *Bharatiyar Charithiram*. Bharati had attended the meeting of the Indian Congress in Calcutta and, on his return journey to south India, he had the opportunity to meet Sister Nivedita. Upon meeting him, she asked Bharati why he had not brought his wife to the Congress meeting. Bharati apparently replied: 'We do not usually take our wives to public meetings; moreover, what use would it be to bring her to the

Indian Congress?' Sister Nivedita urged Bharati to recognize women's right to freedom and their fundamental equality with men.

Bharati's extraordinary commitment to women's freedom reflected his all-consuming passion for the sacred ideal of *human* freedom. Bharati's love of freedom completely infused his thinking about everything that interested him—purifying him spiritually and bringing outstanding intellectual clarity to his meditations on life and the world. In this sense, the oppression of women was one specific manifestation of the broader problem of human oppression that concerned the poet.

These connections emerge clearly in the first essay of this group, 'The Place of Woman'. Here, Bharati makes two key points. First, he identifies violence as the root of men's domination of women, not only in India, but also throughout the world—and, in the broader context of male domination of the female, even in nature. He ascribes to women, not an 'inability' to respond to violence with violence, but, instead, an unwillingness to do so because of what he characterizes as woman's essentially loving nature and, hence, her greater spiritual refinement. Secondly, Bharati makes a potent analogy between his call to men to liberate women from their oppression and his demand that the British should liberate India. Domination is domination, he says; and, whatever the context, the urge to dominate one's fellow human beings must be utterly relinquished.

Finally, in 'Women's Freedom', Bharati addresses a fundamental and disturbing issue: men's desire to control women's sexuality. This has always been a widely accepted rationale for the suppression of women's freedom. Bharati denounces it as irrational. Strikingly, he comments that 'chastity . . . is not everything in life'. With wonderful insight, he observes, 'Indeed, no single virtue can be made to do duty for the infinite realizations of a liberated human existence.' No rote social morality could satisfy Bharati's desire for truth. This, too, reflected his love of freedom—mental freedom, freedom of the imagination.

Chapter 18: The Place of Woman

1. The deities referred to by Bharati are Parvati, Siva's consort, Lakshmi, goddess of wealth, Brahma, the creator ("the four-faced Father of the Worlds"), and Saraswati, goddess of knowledge.

2. Lord Curzon (1859–1925) was Viceroy of India from 1899 to 1905. Interestingly, he was firmly against women's suffrage in Great Britain and attempted, unsuccessfully, to prevent the passage of legislation granting the vote to women. He felt that allowing women to vote would 'lead to the disruption and even to the ruin of the Empire'. Quoted by Penelope Tuson, 'Lord Curzon's Anti-Suffrage Appeal' 4 June 2013, on the British Library 'Untold Lives' Blog, available at http://britishlibrary.typepad.co.uk/untoldlives/2013/06/lord-curzons-anti-suffrage-appeal.html (last visited 25 Jan. 2021). David Lloyd George (1863–1945) was Prime Minister of Britain from 1916 to 1922, leading the country during the first World War.

Chapter 19: Women's Freedom

1. These women were Vedic philosophers. For an interesting overview, see Subhamoy Das, 'Four Famous Female Figures of Vedic India: About Ghosha, Lopamudra, Maitreyi and Gargi' *available at http://hinduism.about.com/od/history/a/ghosha_lopamudra_ maitreyi_gargi.htm* (last visited 5 Aug. 2020).

2. In the following essay and translations, Andal is introduced by Bharati himself; there is more than one poetess known as Avvai in Tamil literature, but Bharati is specifically referring to the author of 'Aathichudi', a guide to moral conduct organized in alphabetical order. Bharati also wrote his own '*Pudiya Aathichudi*' ('New Aathichudi').

Chapter 21: The Crime of Caste

The extent of Bharati's commitment to caste equality cannot possibly be overstated. It can be meaningfully compared only to his practically innate and intrinsic commitment to women's rights. No Indian reformer before or since has ever been more convinced, not only of the equality of castes, but also of the need to bring the different castes together in the everyday functioning of Indian society.

Noteworthy in this article is Bharati's characteristic and severe criticism of the Brahmin community—his own. The Brahmins, he felt, had failed to uphold the important values of education, learning, and intellect which they had historically developed, and which it was their duty to share with society at large. Bharati's solutions to caste prejudice are as practical as they are radical: to eat together and to promote intermarriage between castes. Similar solutions are surely needed to overcome racial and ethnic prejudice everywhere.

It is important to note that Bharati not only wrote about these ideas, but he also put them into practice in his own life. While staying in Kadayam, Chellamma's village, his experiments with inter-caste commensality—sharing meals with his non-Brahmin friends and followers—notably led to his expulsion from the Brahmin community.

Bharati's advocacy of caste equality drew the attention of Sri C. Rajagopalachari, the first Governor-General of independent India. In an article entitled 'A Living Poet and Social Reformer', also published in *Commonweal* in the October 20, 1916 issue, Rajaji writes:

> The worth of the remarkable poet of Madras has not been at all sufficiently recognized by the people, for love of whom he has made irrevocable and unmeasured sacrifice. The call of the Mother has been so well heard by this poet that the false love that misleads other and lesser men does not mislead him.
>
> To those who have followed the writings of Mr. Subramania Bharati there is nothing new in the views expressed in his recent article against caste, an institution with

which some of our other Nationalists are so pleased and our lost faith in which they seek to revive. The article is a useful contribution to our literature in its attitude towards social reform.

Chapter 22: Love and Marriage

Bharati was firmly opposed to the tradition of child-marriage, which he considered barbaric. His sensitive and poetic nature also led him to disapprove of 'arranged' marriage in the usual sense of the term. Instead, he looks to nature for guidance on how to approach this aspect of human life, and draws from nature's example to argue for independence and self-determination in the choice of life-partner.

He attempted to put this doctrine into practice in the life of his elder daughter, Thangammal, initially refusing to find her a bridegroom and arguing that she should be married in due course to a German prince. His dream did not come to pass quite like this, as other members of the family intervened. But the chosen youth was respectful of his father-in-law to be, and Bharati himself officiated at his daughter's wedding.

Part III: Philosophical Essays

Chapter 23: The Dawn

In this essay, Bharati's qualities as a Renaissance poet come to the fore. Renaissance thinkers and writers present a unique literary category: their individual gifts combine with historical forces to inspire broad cultural regeneration in societies as a whole. Individuals like these may appear at turning points in the history of societies and civilizations. In Bharati's case, the historical forces generated by the Indian independence movement arguably transformed him into one of these historic leaders of human development.

The well from which Bharati drew his inspiration was, in fact, an ocean—the ocean of ancient Vedic thought, which he read and imbibed, and essentially recreated in modern form in his own poetry. The visionary aspect of Vedic literature had a deep impact on Bharati. His poetry reflects the qualities that he saw in the poems of the Vedic 'seers': clarity, linguistic abundance and richness, simultaneous exploration and veneration of nature, and universality of themes and values. Bharati's conception of life as reflected in his poetry was extraordinarily comprehensive, especially by the Indian and Western standards of his day. No aspect of human life and experience was unworthy of the poet's attention or beyond the reach of his imagination.

As Bharati's opening sentence in this essay reveals, the Renaissance that he hoped for, dreamed of, and worked tirelessly towards—that he 'visualized', in the purest sense of the word—was also comprehensive. National regeneration not only meant renewal of the country; it also signified social and individual regeneration, psychological and spiritual rebirth.

1. Agni is the ancient Vedic god of fire. Bharati goes on to talk about the 'fire' in each person as an expression of his or her 'higher Will'. The significance and symbolism of Agni was extremely important to Bharati and appears in some of his mystical poems in Tamil, including '*Agni Kunju*' ('A Tiny Flame') and '*Velvi Pattu*' ('The Fire Sacrifice').

Chapter 24: Rasa

This article deserves to be recognized as one of the true gems of Bharati's output in English. In his analysis of the single 'key word', rasa, Bharati is able to convey the essential attitudes of Indian culture with simplicity, directness, and elegance. The key idea of Renaissance reappears; once again, national Renaissance is mirrored by spiritual regeneration at the individual level, culminating in the assertion, at once tantalizing and inspiring, that 'The trembling coward is wasting the material which can be utilized for making himself a hero.'

Characteristically, the essay ends with a call to action and the poet's exhortation to his fellows (and to himself) to choose action, and to attain godliness—empowerment and immortality —through our acts.

Chapter 25: Immortality

Bharati was preoccupied with immortality. His philosophical conviction in this regard gave birth to a unique ambition—the desire to live forever, not only in spirit, but also in the physical body. In this pursuit, Bharati's experiences were extraordinary, even overwhelming. He sought help from the community of *siddhas,* holy men, whom he came to know when he lived in Pondicherry. Among these was his guru, Kullachami, a siddha and a *gnani,* a man of learning and true wisdom.

Bharati writes that, by various means, Kullachami showed him the path to 'eternity': 'a root of the *Vedanta* tree.' Bharati was also close to other *yogis* in Pondicherry, such as Govindasamy, and the Swamy from Jaffna; they were even able to make it possible for him to 'see' his deceased father and mother.

Indeed, Bharati proclaimed that he himself was a siddha, and that he had come to this world to create a 'society of the gods' *(amarar sangham).* Indra, the Vedic leader of the gods, gave him the strength of mind to destroy evil, while Surya, the Sun, blessed him with the light of the intellect, and Varuna, the Wind, would grant him long life. With the help of these Powers, Bharati announced that he would establish Krita-yuga, a Heavenly life, in this world.

The poet died prematurely at the age of thirty-eight. In a mystical sense, it can still be said that he fulfilled the prophecy in this essay. His poetry clearly reflects the experience of 'flinging myself into the blazing fire of universal Reality', and he is indeed lost in the Supreme Light, thereby achieving 'immortality'. ...No further comment can be made.

1. These are references to Krishna, made very much in the traditional poetical style of the Tamils, by painting the picture of the Lord and identifying Him indirectly, through His attributes. Bharati was a master in the use of such poetic imagery, gleaned from his deep familiarity with the Puranas, India's sacred myths, as well as myriad other sources of Indian cultural and religious imagery known to him.

Chapter 26: To the Being of the Universe

This essay was most probably an unpublished piece. In both form and content, it can be considered a kind of '*mantra*', a prayer addressed to the 'Being of the Universe' in which Bharati surrenders his fears and seeks 'assurance of victory over death and sorrow'. Written by the poet in the free flow of his thoughts, it reveals Bharati's preoccupation with observing and controlling his own psychological propensities— the inner movements of his mind. In this, he participates in a great philosophical tradition that is characteristically Indian, and perhaps Eastern, though not uniquely so. Most of Bharati's usual concerns are apparent here: his desire for immortality, which he believed to be possible even in the purely physical sense of living forever in the body; his belief that illness and death are occasioned by 'nervous shocks' that destroy physical and mental health; and his unwavering reliance on the principle of love as the secret to self-perfection and an ideal life. In Bharati's thought, love always serves to unify the individual with the divine spirit of the cosmos.

In his poem *Bharati Arubattaru* ('Bharati Sixty Six'), Bharati also talks about the means of overcoming death based on the scientific theories developed by the pioneering Indian scientist (and science fiction writer in the Bengali language) Dr Jagdish Chandra Bose (1858–1937).

This psychologically revealing essay also demonstrates Bharati's reliance on the supremacy of 'Will' over mind. In other words, the poet believed the mind to be profoundly malleable to the direction of

its owner—'passive clay in the Almighty hands of Will'—and points
out that thoughts themselves are 'the architects of life'. Once again, he
emphasizes the need to take control of the propensities and activities
of the mind to lead a successful life.

1. Bharati's use of this extremely colloquial expression seems quite
    deliberate. This section exudes the poet's impatience with so-
    called 'traditions' that impede the (immediate) establishment of
    a just and beautiful society.
2. Sri Ramanuja Acharya (1017–1137) is considered the greatest
    of all Vaishnavite philosopher-saints and a leading proponent of
    Advaita philosophy, which advances the principle of the unity
    of all beings and, perhaps the same thing, the identity of every
    being with the Divine. As illustrated by this essay, Bharati was a
    profound devotee and exponent of Advaita.
3. The theory that 'nervous shocks' ultimately cause the death of
    the human organism originates with Jagdish Chandra Bose: see
    Chapter 26, 'To the Being of the Universe', above. Bharati's
    general attitude to modern science was highly positive and his
    poetry in Tamil is filled with references to the cosmos and natural
    phenomena in surprisingly 'scientific' language. Of course,
    the inspiration of the Vedic seers is also apparent in Bharati's
    fascination with the natural world.

Chapter 27: The Service of God

1. Annie Besant (1847–1933) was a British social reformer who
    eventually settled in India and became a supporter of the
    National Movement. She established the Indian Home Rule
    League in 1916 and was its first president, and she was also
    a member of the Indian National Congress. Besant became
    President of the Theosophical Society in 1907. See Notes on
    Chapter 8, 'The Fox with the Golden Tail', above. The BBC

has a short biography of Besant, available at http://www.bbc.co.uk/history/historic_figures/besant_annie.shtml (last visited 5 Aug. 2020).

2. *Soma* was the intoxicating liquor consumed by the Aryans of Vedic times. In *The Story of India* Michael Wood journeys to the Russian steppe and attempts to make and consume soma according to the descriptions of the ancient texts! See Introduction, above, note 3.

3. The references here will be obvious to every Indian, the mythology surrounding the life of Lord Krishna and the story of the Pandava brothers immortalized in the great Sanskrit epic of Vyasa, the *Mahabharata*.

4. A reference to the story of Sugreeva, lord of the monkeys, in the ancient Sanskrit epic, the *Ramayana*.

5. The *Upanishads* distinguish between '*preya*', the pleasurable, and 'shreya', a fundamentally untranslateable word that can be expressed in English as the beneficial, or the ultimate good. The choice of shreya is favored by the righteous, as it promotes the 'attainment of that which is not already possessed' and 'the preservation of that which is already in possession'. See H.C. Ganguli, *Fear of Death and the Bhagavad Gita*, with a Foreword by Professor G. Misra (Global Vision Publishing House, New Delhi 2008), 30–32.

6. The Vedic gods of Fire, Agni (*gnana shakti*) and Water (or Oceans), Varuna.

7. The goddess Durga, when worshipped as Kali, takes on a wild aspect that has historically been interpreted by certain cults as Bharati describes. In south India, the two 'faces' of Shakti are the peaceful Parvati and the furious Kali; for example, the two manifestations can be viewed facing each other in the *Thillai Kali* temple in the famous temple city of Chidambaram.

8. Once again, Bharati alludes to one of his fundamental ideas here, questioning the redemptive power of suffering. He agrees

that suffering can be redemptive; but it is not the only means of spiritual growth. For Bharati, suffering is never the preferred route to enlightenment.

9. The previous publication of this essay reads 'plunging into high'. The phrase must have been printed in error, but it is impossible to know what Bharati's original was. The words 'soaring to the heights' have been substituted as approximating Bharati's evident meaning.

Chapter 28: The Siddha and the Superman

In this fascinating essay, Bharati confronts one of the key philosophical ideas of his time: Friedrich Nietzsche (1844–1900) and his ideal of the 'Superman'. Nietzsche's work introducing the *Übermensch*, 'Thus Spoke Zarathustra', was first published in English translation in 1896, three years after its appearance in German; the term 'Superman' first appears in translation in 1909.

Bharati's remarks are prescient in two senses. First, he was quick to grasp the importance of the concept, which he rightly saw as a key archetype of modern Western civilization. Secondly, he sensed the danger inherent in it, as the Superman not only rejected the intellectual restraints and perceived passivity of Christianity, but also, developed a seductive and radical vision of human action. The ends of the Superman would justify his means.

The idea haunted Bharati and he returns to it in many of his English writings. As Bharati points out in this essay, the key achievement of the Superman is the attainment of power—a goal of limited significance and a potential threat to harmonious co-existence with one's fellow beings, human and otherwise. Bharati's philosophical viewpoint was that of a kind of 'citizen of the universe' and his true ambition, Vedic in scope, was to perceive and understand the reality of the cosmos as a whole. He describes his vision of an ideal life as one based on the attainment of harmony between individual life and cosmic purpose. Bharati's siddha is therefore a very different person from the Superman. He (also she) stands for ideals that Bharati held very dear— egalitarianism, humanism, and the opportunity to overcome the obvious limitations of individual selfhood through vision, devotion, and compassion. As an Indian nationalist and reformer, Bharati's reckoning with the Superman offers an occasion to affirm the inherent value of the Indian perspective on life, and to point out that India has an important cultural contribution to make in a world faced with growing political and moral turmoil.

The purpose of these remarks is to provide a context for Bharati's essay; criticism of Nietzsche's immensely influential writings is beyond their scope. Still, it should be noted that Nietzsche's legacy has been widely subject to misinterpretation and abuse. As Professor Bernd Magnus comments, 'Although he was an ardent foe of nationalism, anti-Semitism, and power politics, his name was later invoked by fascists to advance the very things he loathed.' (https://www.britannica. com/biography/Friedrich-Nietzsche, last visited 27 Jan. 2021).

1. Thomas Carlyle (1795–1881), Scottish philosopher with strong Romantic sympathies whose reputation declined due to his controversial writing on race (e.g. 'Occasional Discourse on the Negro Question'); among the contributions that ensured his status in the nineteenth century were his writings on heroism and his role in bringing German literature, including Goethe, to a British audience through his scholarship and translations. See e.g. https://www.britannica.com/biography/Thomas-Carlyle.
2. Here, by *Shastras,* Bharati means the codes of Hindu law.

Chapter 29: Fatalism

In this exquisite essay, Bharati addresses one of the grandest of all themes: the relationship between fate and free will. The question preoccupies him as a poet and philosopher, but also as a nationalist who seeks to examine one of the bases for the West's claims of so-called 'superiority' over the East. With typical clarity of mind, he observes that human beings are part of their environment, in other words, Nature; and, for him, Nature is synonymous with Parashakti. Rather than seeking to reconcile fate and freedom, Bharati adopts a beautifully Indian approach, showing how these apparent contradictions can exist in their own, unique balance.

1. The men Bharati names are well known figures in Indian history. Chandragupta was the 'founder of the Mauryan dynasty (reigned *c.* 321–*c.* 297 BCE) and the first emperor to unify most of India under one administration': his extraordinary life is described in the Encyclopedia Britannica, https://www.britannica.com/biography/Chandragupta (last visited 26 Jan. 2021). The story of Vikramaditya, a legendary ancient Indian emperor famed for encouraging Sanskrit scholarship at his court, is difficult to verify, with competing versions arguing about whether he was man or myth: see e.g. https://www.newworldencyclopedia.org/entry/Vikram%C4%81ditya and Wikipedia's interesting entry on this figure (last visited 26 Jan. 2021). Akbar, Mughal emperor from 155 to 1605, was famed for espousing religious tolerance and encouraging culture (see e.g. Kenneth A. Ballhatchet, 'Akbar' in Encyclopedia Britannica, https://www.britannica.com/biography/Akbar, last visited 26 Jan. 2021). Shivaji (1630–80) was the founder of the Martha empire in Western India, a Hindu who resisted Muslim oppression but also supported religious tolerance; see the excellent article by Ranjit Ramachandra Desai, 'Shivaji,' in Encyclopedia Britannica, https://www.britannica.com/biography/Shivaji, last visited 26 Jan. 2021).

2. Shankara, 'renowned exponent of the Advaita Vedanta school of philosophy', who lived during the eighth century: see e.g. https://www.britannica.com/biography/Shankara.

Chapter 30: Blunting the Imagination

1. Swami Ramatirtha (1873–1906) was a scholar of Vedanta philosophy who followed in the footsteps of Swami Vivekananda (see Chapter 9, 'Reflections', above) to travel and teach around the world, particularly in the United States. A meeting with Swami Vivekananda apparently inspired him to give up family and career (as a professor of mathematics), and become a sanyasi. On Tagore, see Chapter 9, 'Reflections' above. Jamsetji Nusserwanji Tata (1839–1904) was a pioneering Indian industrialist; today, the Tata company remains one of India's (and the world's) leading corporations (see e.g. tata.com, last visited 27 Jan. 2020). Bharati's list of notable Indians shows that he valued many kinds of social contributions—spiritual, artistic, and industrial—traditional and modern. Bharati's own father, Chinnasamy Iyer, had attempted to establish a cotton industry in south India; but his efforts were frustrated by the British, ultimately leading to his financial ruin and death.

2. The Bhashyas that Bharati refers to are, in particular, commentaries on Sanskrit religious texts.

3. *Vairagis,* those who are practitioners of *vairagya,* refers to the art of mental discipline as described in Patanjali's *Yoga Sutra.* The issue of control of the mind, as is evidenced by the essays here, was one of Bharati's deepest preoccupations.

4. Bharati, indeed, paraphrases John Ruskin (1819–1900), the extraordinarily influential critic, writer, and artist. Among other achievements, Ruskin became the first Slade Professor of Fine Art at the University of Oxford, where he founded the Ruskin School of Drawing and Fine Art. Ruskin delivered a series of three lectures that were published in an 1866 collection, *The Crown of Wild Olive.* The words recalled by Bharati are as follows: 'Half-a-dozen men, with one day's work, could cleanse those pools, and trim the flowers about their banks, and make every breath of summer air above them

rich with cool balm; and every glittering wave medicinal, as if it ran, troubled of angels, from the porch of Bethesda.'

Chapter 31: Some Political Maxims

It is easy to see what appealed to Bharati about this list of 'maxims', an intriguing mixture of common sense, shrewdness, and noble insight. It is worth reading them alongside his articles about the conduct of the British government in India. By contrast, the emphasis on truth, fairness, and accountability in government reflected by these 'maxims' must have struck a chord.

1.   Doctor of Islamic law; imam who leads prayers in a mosque. See e.g. Merriam-Webster dictionary, https://www.merriam-webster. com/dictionary/maulvi, or Oxford dictionaries online, https:// www.lexico.com/en/definition/moulvi.

Part IV: Language and Literature

Chapter 32: 'Vernaculars'

This short article contains some extraordinarily important ideas. Once again, Bharati is ahead of his time. Here, he is engaged in an exercise that is still not usual in literary circles worldwide, though it should be: considering the literatures of non-Western languages in an objective light and seeking to assess them from a relatively unbiased point of view. The modern dominance of the English language effectively impedes those who wish to engage in this exercise or, at the very last, advocate for it. English is so widespread that there is arguably a tendency to assume that major works are either written in English or available in translation. Similarly, the volume of material published in English is so great that one could never read all of it in a lifetime, or even in several lifetimes.

All of this distracts from the point rightfully made by Bharati. English is a modern language; its pedigree can be traced back by about two thousand years, to the epic poem Beowulf, but the Old English in which the poem was composed is largely incomprehensible to the lay reader now. Tamil, in contrast, is one of the world's ancient languages. Historian Michael Wood refers to Tamil as the world's oldest classical language, and the literary language has been in use, more or less consistently, from ancient times until the present. Modern Tamil grammer continues to rely on the oldest existing grammatical text, Tolkappiyam, whose dating is controversial, but which is usually considered to be between 1700 and 2100 years old. Bharati lists important classics of Tamil literature (and there are still others that he could have noted besides). These works, or parts of them, may occasionally be available in translation, but it is probably fair to say that translations have not yet succeeded in conveying their stature to a world readership, much less secured their general recognition as literary masterpieces on par with those in English, French, and German (or, indeed, in other languages of international literary 'prestige', such as Russian). The need for translation is itself a reflection of economic factors and, of course, the colonial legacy, which not only spread the English (and French) languages around the world, but also assured the status of these languages as the tongues of conquerors.

An additional consequence of this global linguistic inequality is the difficulty of learning Tamil today. While some learning materials are available, the serious student of Tamil faces enormous challenges that a student of any European language could not even imagine. Where are the books or methods for non-native speakers to learn the basics of Tamil grammar or to acquire sufficient vocabulary to read independently the important writers of the Tamil tradition—including Bharati himself? Some material is available, but is it enough? The problem is particularly apparent in the Tamil diaspora worldwide where, arguably, the only real hope of learning Tamil is to be found in the teaching of children by their parents. At the same time, immigrant families face enormous pressure to function successfully in environments where even speaking the local language with a foreign accent can be a liability. Times are surely changing, but slowly.

By no means could Bharati ever intend his remarks to be seen as negative towards the language or literature of any human culture, as he would have considered all biased attitudes contemptible. Indeed, he personally admired Shelley's poetry so much that he adopted the pen name of 'Shelley *dasan*' at one point for his own writing. Instead, Bharati takes aim at the 'annoying attitude of patronage and condescension when writing and talking about our [Indian] languages'. The extent to which such attitudes have changed, even today, is debatable, and it could also be argued that the problem afflicts Indian literature at large—not only the extensive classical (and modern) literature of the Tamils. It remains a heavy and persistent legacy of the colonial past.

1. Bharati objected deeply to the British practice of referring to Indian languages as 'vernaculars', as is apparent in this comment (where Bharati places the offensive term in quotations) and in the letter that follows (where he treats the use of 'vernacular' to refer to Indian languages as a simple error, followed by the Latin 'sic'). As is discussed in the accompanying note, Bharati felt that it was plainly incorrect to call Indian languages vernaculars because of their antiquity and distinguished literary traditions. He was incensed that the term would be used for these languages to distinguish them from the commonly spoken languages of Europe, to the extent that he feels compelled to point out (unusually for him, given his fundamental rejection of cultural chauvinism) that comparisons between the two groups might actually favor the stature of Indian languages over their European counterparts. His comments highlight the extreme seriousness of the issue. It is also interesting to adopt Bharati's own methodology and consider the etymological roots of the word 'vernacular', which lie in the Latin word *verna*, meaning

'home-born slave': see *Oxford Dictionary of English Etymology,* ed. C.T. Onions with the assistance of G.W.S. Friiedrichsen and R.W. Furchfield (Oxford University Press, Oxford 1996).

2. Tiruvalluvar's ancient text addresses virtually every aspect of human experience in the pithy form of couplets, known as 'kurals' The text is of indeterminate date but may have been written around the second century BCE.

3. The Ramayana, the life of King Rama and his wife Sita, was originally a Sanskrit epic authored by the sage Valmiki. It is considered one of the foundational texts of Indian culture (the other being the Mahabharata, Vyasa's epic which, legend has it, was written down by no less a scribe than Lord Ganesh). The Ramayana was subsequently 'retold' by outstanding poets in many of India's national languages. Kamban's *Ramayana* dates from the twelfth century and is sublimely adapted to the culture of south India. Kamban lived from about 1180 to 1250.

4. *Silappadhikaram* is one of the five Tamil 'epics'that give Tamil its renown as a language of epics. Its author, Ilango Adigal, was a Jain poet of the second century. The work has an egalitarian and democratic theme (so much for 'Asiatic' despotism), as a woman of the city calls the King to account for a grevious act of injustice. Bharati, in his turn, wrote *Panchali Sabadham* ('Panchali's Vow'), a dramatic retelling of a famous incident from the Mahabharata which is now considered a modern 'Tamil epic' in this very tradition.

Chapter 33: National Languages as Media of Instruction

This essay seems curiously relevant to the present time. Bharati objected to the devaluation of Tamil and other national languages in India, and to what he saw as a danger that the people of India would be dispossessed of their own cultures by the removal of native languages from children's education. The rationale for doing so was apparently the unsuitability of Indian languages for dealing with science—a bizarre contention, considering that Indians had made important contributions to scientific knowledge from ancient times. The solution that Bharati proposes is an interesting one: the needs of modern science, he argues, could be filled in India by a combination of native languages and recourse to Sanskrit, just as classical Latin and Greek have served similar functions in Europe.

In independent India, however, the sequel to these debates has been singularly strange. The search for a national language, paradoxically but perhaps inevitably, led to conflict between Hindi and so-called 'regional' languages like Tamil. Ironically, the proficiency of Indians in English, the modern global language, is now considered to be one of the factors that has enabled India to become a major economic power in the modern (post-colonial) world.

Bharati, it should be noted, spoke excellent Hindi as well as English, having completed his education in Benares, and he studied Sanskrit as well as classical Tamil literature. How would the passionate poet have viewed the post-Independence turn of events? The current dominance of English hardly disproves any of his arguments.

1. *The Hindu* continues to be published today, as 'India's National Newspaper'. It is based in Chennai, formerly Madras.

Part V: Tamil Tradition & Translations

Chapter 34: The Occult Element in Tamil Speech

Here we see Bharati in a more esoteric, yet captivating mood—showing his fascination with a peculiar form of 'etymology'. As a poet who was to develop a newly modern approach to the Tamil language, it is hardly surprising that Bharati dwells on the capacity of the language to convey deeper and more varied meanings than the literal, more superficial sense of words. He enjoys the shades of meaning hidden within the language and exploits them fully.

The spiritual 'guru' that Bharati refers to in this essay was his Pondicherry friend Kullachami (see also note on Chapter 25, 'Immortality', above). Kullachami was a sanyasi, a holy ascetic, and a 'seer'. Bharati writes about him in his autobiographical poem, *Bharati Arubattaru,* as well as in his stories and articles. Kullachami's spiritual teaching unfolded through his own 'extraordinary' behaviour and perhaps, through his use of occult speech. Bharati may well have learned about the occult aspects of Tamil from Kullachami and the other sanyasis whom he knew in Pondicherry.

Bharati says that he hopes to write further on this theme but, sadly, he never did. This is his only English essay on the subject.

1. The Oxford English Dictionary defines the word 'occult' as follows: 'involving or relating to mystical, supernatural, or magical powers, practices, or phenomena: an occult ceremony'. Bharati's particular focus is on the intrinsic yet hidden spiritual dimension of Tamil speech, as becomes clear in this essay.

2. Literally, one who practices 'yoga', not in the modern Western sense, but in the original Indian sense of mental, spiritual, and physical disciplines leading to enlightenment; the *yogi* was a spiritually advanced man (*yogini* for a similarly accomplished woman).

3. Thayumanavar (1706–42) was a Tamil poet, philosopher, and saint who promulgated the *Saiva Siddhanta* philosophy of Siva-worship in south India. Bharati greatly admired him.

Chapter 35: Andal, the Vaishnava Poetess

Andal was one of twelve south Indian saints, known as the Alwars. She wanted to marry the Lord, just as Mira Bai, the North Indian poetess, wanted to become the bride of Krishna. Andal's literary works are *Tiruppavai,* a collection of thirty poems, and *Nachiar Thirumozhi,* a poem of 143 stanzas. According to legend, the Lord appeared to Andal's father in a dream and told him that He would marry Andal at the famed Srirangam temple. Accordingly, she went to Srirangam and, as described by Bharati, is said to have merged with the Lord.

Bharati has translated three of Andal's poems: 'To the Cuckoo', 'I Dreamed a Dream', and 'Ye Others'.

Bharati was profoundly drawn to the Alwars' intensely personal experiences of the Divine. He shared their sense of Divine manifestation in human relations; but his experience was also different from that of the Alwars in the sense that his vision is Advaitic in nature. Advaita means the unity of all beings and, even further, their unity with God. In Bharati's experience, 'all forms of human life and emotion and all phenomena of the universe' are the 'forms' of Parashakti. Upon these heights of Advaita mysticism, God and human are one and the same. In contrast, Bharati describes the Vaishnava experience as an awareness that all beings and all human relations are 'symbols' and 'means' to reaching the Divine—'stepping stones' to 'grasp the Supreme', rather than the Supreme Herself (or Himself).

Andal came to be known as 'Nachiar' the name by which Bharati refers to her in the following translations.

1. See discussion of Tagore in Chapter 9, Reflections, above, and accompanying note.

2. The Pandyas were kings who ruled in south India in the fifth century, when the southern tip of the Indian subcontinent was divided into three kingdoms, Chera (roughly, the borderlands with modern Kerala), Chola (south-eastern Tamil Nadu), and Pandya (the deep south, ultimately associated with Madurai as their capital and builders of the famed Madurai Meenakshi temple).

3. In Hindu mythological tradition, cosmic time is divided into yugas, each several hundreds of millions of years long. Kali is the yuga, or period, of social and cultural decline. Bharati always argued for the revival of Krita-yuga, a period of ascendancy and

greatness; and, indeed, the explicitly stated aim of his poetry was to recreate the Krita-yuga. '*Nalla kalam varuhithu*,' he wrote, with passionate eagerness—the time of good things, the era of greatness, is coming! So it is hardly surprising that Bharati rejects the very existence of Kali Yuga in this essay, commenting, with breathtaking simplicity, that 'we need not believe' in it.

4. Bharati means the twelve Alwars, Tamil saints in the Vaishnavite tradition.

5. The Vishnu temple at Srirangam is one of the great temple complexes of south India. In his form as Sri Ranganatha Swamy, Vishnu reclines in the sanctum sanctorum.

Chapter 36: To the Cuckoo

Simple, direct, and memorable phrases convey the splendour of Andal's spiritual experience with almost physical vitality. Bharati's immersion in Andal's words is absolute; he forgets himself. By a paradox, the simplicity of Bharati's language, a kind of self-effacement practiced in the art of translation, also paints an absolutely accurate portrait of him, as artist and man.

1. An Indian flower famous for its scent; see e.g. Matt Ritter, 'Striving for Diversity: Fragrant Champaca', Pacific Horticulture Society, April 2012, https://www.pacifichorticulture.org/articles/striving-for-diversity-fragrant-champaca (last visited 26 Feb. 2021).

Chapter 39: Nammalwar, the Supreme Vaishnava Saint and Poet

This essay is an introduction to Bharati's English translation of Nammalwar's poetry from *Tiruvaymoli* ('The Sacred Utterance'), a poem composed of more than a thousand stanzas and acclaimed as Nammalwar's masterpiece. The three poems translated into English by Bharati are 'The Gospel of Spiritual Freedom', 'Love-Mad', and 'Hymn of the Golden Age'.

Bharati's critique of Nammalwar as a writer of great 'inequality', whom he still venerates, could only be expressed by an outstanding poet. His comments here show the depth of his reading in Tamil, and the care with which he studied and meditated upon the works of classic Tamil poets who came before him. His appreciation is keen on all levels—literary, philosophical, and mystical. Bharati's relationship to the poetic tradition that he inherited echoes T.S. Eliot's celebrated essay 'Tradition and the Individual Talent':

> Tradition is a matter of much wider significance . . . the historical sense involves a perception, not only of the pastness of the past, but of its presence; the historical sense compels a man to write not merely with his own generation in his bones, but with a feeling that the whole of the literature of Europe from Homer and within it the whole of the literature of his own country has a simultaneous existence and composes a simultaneous order . . . And it is at the same time what makes a writer most acutely conscious of his place in time, of his contemporaneity.

1. This word is difficult to translate; it can mean concentration, meditation, contemplation, trance. Monier-Williams' Sanskrit-English Dictionary lists various meanings: 'concentration of the thoughts', 'profound or abstract meditation', 'intense contemplation'. See Monier Monier-Williams, *A Sanskrit-English Dictionary*, New Edition by E. Leumann, C. Cappeller, and others (Oxford, Clarendon Press, Reprinted 2006; originally published 1899), vol. 2, p. 1159.

2. In his own footnote, Bharati notes: 'The form of the Question reminds one of Epictetus' definition of man, 'Thou art a little soul carrying about a corpse.' Swinburne (1837-1909) adapted

the saying in his poem Hymn to Proserpine (1866): 'A little soul for a little bears up this corpse which is man.'

3. Here, Bharati refers to the other Alwars as being embodiments of the mythological accoutrements of the Deity as opposed to the Deity himself.

4. Bharati prefers this spelling to the transliteration now accepted by linguists, of the Tamil letter 'zh', *(Tiruvaymozhi)*—which, indeed, sounds nothing like 'zh' as used in Russian for example, which English speakers are more accustomed to seeing.

Chapter 40: Love-Mad

The Vedic sages perceived that 'all is God'. The Vaishnavas, devotees of Lord Vishnu—known to Hindus as the 'Preserver', who is incarnated on Earth for the salvation of humanity in the form of *avatars* such as Krishna and Rama—followed in this tradition. They called nature, prakriti, the body of Vishnu, and the 'life' that pervades nature, the soul, *atma,* of Vishnu.

The Vaishnava poets are so entirely immersed in the 'ocean of love' that is Vishnu that their poetry is replete with Vishnu legends. The passionate quality of their devotion is unique. S. Vijaya Bharati writes that 'their hearts melt when they hear the name of Vishnu, filled with wonder and joy. The spiritual relationship with Vishnu first expressed by the Vedic poets continued throughout the centuries and informed the experience of the Vaishnava poets in their turn.

The ten incarnations of Mahavishnu ('Thoughts') explain that these *avataras* accomplished specific goals: the destruction of evil forces and the maintenance of a peaceful and happy world.

S. Vijaya Bharati comments: 'Lord Vishnu's names are— Narayana, Govinda, Madhava; His cities—Dwaraka, Mathura, the Venkata hill; His banner—the mighty golden Eagle; His Discus is the arm with which he drives away evil; He reposes on the Serpent

Adisesha of the thousand hoods; His garland is the fragrant Tulsi; His Conch and His sea-hued colour identify Him.'

The deeds of Vishnu's avataras are renowned and celebrated incidents, well known to the popular imagination throughout India, South and North. These many legends, in all their wondrous details, became a part of the experience of the Alwars, who looked upon them with admiration and devotion, and re-worked them to ascend the heights of ecstatic experience in their re-tellings and re-imaginings. The poetry of the Alwars speaks of humanity's love for God and, as such, it is universal. But knowing the legends enormously enriches our understanding of the Alwars' experience, allowing us to enjoy their poetry even more.

Chapter 43: Hymns to Kumara: The Son of God

Arunagiri Nathar was a Tamil poet and saint of the fifteenth century. He was a devotee of Murugan (Kumara), the Hindu god who is the son of Parvati and Shiva. Murugan represents beauty; he is also the Lord of War and Victory. The Vedas describe him as the son of Agni, the fire-god; the *puranas* describe the mythology of Murugan and his deeds; and the Tamil poets of the Sangam period (400–50 AD), particularly Nakkirar's poem *Tirumurugarruppadai*, shows the way of wisdom by following the path that leads through the six abodes of Murugan, holy sites in Tamil Nadu associated with Murugan where Murugan temples have been built.

Arunagiri's poems are remarkable in their poetic structure, characterized by beautiful musical qualities and philosophical depth.

Part VI: Bharati's Translations of His Tamil Originals

Chapter 44: Agni

This poem is a partial translation of a Tamil original. The original poem is structured as a drama in which the *rishis* (sages) ignite the fire at the altar and sing the praises of Agni, while the *asuras* (demons) moan and raise lamentations at the sight of the Sacrificial Fire. The poem was sung by Bharati to an extraordinary melody. Bharati has only translated the first set of stanzas—the singing of the Vedic rishis but not the lamentations of the asuras.

The original poem is a masterpiece that was inspired by Bharati's study of the Vedas. His spiritual writings include *Vedarishigalin Kavithai* ('The Poetry of the Vedic Rishis'), in which he translates the Rigveda and writes an introduction to these ancient verses, explaining the essence of some of the *mantras* that describe the never-ending battle of the *devas* (immortals) with the asuras which has been in progress since time immemorial. S. Vijaya Bharati comments: 'In his Tamil poem, the Sacrificial Fire into which the sages pour ghee roars towards the sky and drives the evil spirits away, to far distant forests. This is an allegorical poem about the struggles of the human spirit against evil—in particular, the evils inherent in our own psyche, so richly studied by Bharati— sorrows, worries, fear, and ignorance.'

1. Bharati defines the term 'All-Will' in his essay 'The Siddha and the Superman' (Chapter 28 above), as 'the will pure and simple— the Shakti of God. The Will of the Universe, the All-Will, the Will not merely for Power, but for Being and Loving, the Will that should, in full measure, be realized by man in himself, if he seeks perfection.'

2. These are all references to Vedic gods, whom Bharati identifies here by attribute as well as (or instead of) name.

Chapter 48: Krishna

One of Bharati's most celebrated poetical works is a group of twenty-three Tamil poems on Krishna, published as *Kannan Pattu;* one more of these poems is translated into English by him here under the title 'In Each Other's Arms'. In these poems, Bharati sings of his experience of Krishna as realized in all human relationships, echoing the experience of Andal and other poets in a way that is at once traditional and completely individual.

Chapter 49: The 'Kummi' of Women's Freedom

The 'Kummi' is a traditional folk dance performed by the women of south India, the origin of which probably goes back a few centuries. S. Vijaya Bharati explains, 'The structure and form of the dance and the music are simple. The music is a joy to sing in a group, and the verses are easy to remember.' Bharati's own daughter, Thangammal, is said to have been an enthusiastic and beautiful dancer of the Kummi.

In his celebrated long poem *Kuyil Pattu* ('Song of the Koel'), Bharati writes of his fascination with the folk music and dances of south India's women. The music was generally associated with the work that the women did, such as drawing well-water, threshing rice paddy on a stone implement, and so on. On special occasions, women danced together in circles, clapping their hands to the rhythm of the songs that they were singing.

The theme of this song about a very traditional activity is utterly modern. With typical fervour, Bharati connects national liberation with women's freedom, seeing them as manifestations of one and the same phenomenon.

More generally, both Bharati's Tamil writing and the melodies in which he composed his poems to be sung were deeply influenced by south Indian folk culture. The Tamil in which he writes manages to capture all the poetry of everyday speech within a framework of elegance and refinement. This is among the special talents that we might associate with a Renaissance writer, fashioning literature out of everyday speech.

It is well-known that Bharati's poems were 'songs' following in the Indian tradition of simultaneous composition of poetry and music. There is little scope within this book to discuss Bharati's outstanding talent as a musical composer, but a few words on such an important issue are warranted.

Bharati's approach to music drew heavily upon folk influences. His songs are characterized by melodies that are novel yet simple, and by a perfect correspondence between music and meaning. His poems are often sung or performed by classical musicians in the Carnatic tradition of south India, but they are usually not performed in their original melodies because of their affinity with folk music and perceived 'unsuitability' for a classical music audience. As a result, many of his original melodies are not performed. At the same time, though, the new renditions of Bharati's songs by Carnatic artists are often highly original in their own right.

If Bharati's own melodies were ultimately to be lost, this would be a blow to Indian cultural heritage, and to the Indian public interested in both Bharati's poetry and in music. Ideally, the original melodies should be kept alive while new compositions should also be encouraged. It is therefore to be hoped that the future will bring more opportunities to hear Bharati's songs as he composed them himself, presenting the public with a more complete picture of his talents.

The important work of members of the poet's immediate family in preserving his original compositions should be noted. As mentioned in the Introduction to this book, Bharati originally taught his songs to his wife, Chellamma, and to their two daughters, Thangammal and Shakuntala, thereby establishing an oral tradition of learning his poems in the family. That tradition has been carried on by his grandchildren and great-grandchildren, some of whom have also undertaken the teaching of Bharati's songs in order to keep this precious legacy alive.

Part VII: From Bharati's Journal

Chapter 50: Toil, Toil, Toil

In this and the following poem, 'Thoughts', in what Bharati calls 'Mantras on the Plane of Will', Bharati discusses work as the path to success, and 'toil' for the achievement of power, greatness, and glory. This, essentially, is the *karma yoga* that the *Bhagavad Gita* preaches. While the importance of 'work' (karma) is reiterated in all eighteen chapters of the *Gita*, the third chapter, entitled 'Karmayoga', insists that work must be carried out with 'detachment'—without becoming enmeshed in tangles, desires, worries, doubts, or, of course, any expectations tied to the fruits of one's work.

In his prayer to Parashakti, the 'Supreme Mother of the Universe', Bharati asks to be given the power to work with freedom from prejudice, folly, fear, vanity, and pride, and with his mind ever focused on Her 'holy feet'.

Chapter 51: Thoughts

These fascinating fragments are what now remain of Bharati's 'Journal of Thoughts and Deeds' (1914–18). They reflect his complete immersion in Indian philosophy, and Advaita in particular, revealing his inner mission to develop the extraordinary mental and, indeed, physical disciplines associated with this tradition. Bharati's understanding of life was profoundly shaped by his reading and experience in this area. In a sense, no reader can comment on his writing without a parallel immersion in the ancient traditions in which he was so knowledgeable; at the same time, Bharati's genius was to reveal and recreate these traditions in a modern context, so that his writings serve as a conduit for the reader to the richness of Bharati's own experience.

His 'Mantras on the Plane of Self' reflect Bharati's personal struggles, such as his fight with poverty, as well as his preoccupations – it could also be said, obsessions – with health, mental and physical, death, and immortality. The reader can be left in no doubt about the poet's desires and aspirations, what he valued, and what he thought of as being unimportant. If we look closely, these Mantras contain a number of pure gems of practical advice on how to live successfully.

Bharati's writings show that he had an extraordinary affinity for mystical experience. The intertwining of these apparently disparate threads, the practical and the mystical, within the very core of his personality takes us some way towards an understanding of his genius.

Bharati's practical ideas on society and nation were directly linked to his mystical quest, and flowed out of the visionary experiences that it generated.

It is remarkable that Bharati chose to write about these experiences in a private journal composed in the English language. By doing so, he was participating in a broader historical movement. The period of the early twentieth century was one in which mystical ideas fascinated artists and thinkers around the world, partly as a result of exposure to Indian culture. Mysticism influenced writers like T.S. Eliot and E.M. Forster, musicians and composers like Alexander Scriabin, visual artists like Wassily Kandinsky, and countless others. The role of the Theosophical Society should also be noted. Interest in mysticism experienced a certain flowering associated with that period which it has perhaps not had since. In this sense, Bharati was a product of his times—a fact that is reflected in his writing in English, too—even as he transcended them.

1. Bharati means this quite literally: with Sanskrit mantras as his point of reference, these and following passages seek to build up incantatory layers, not only of words, but also of sounds to bring the person speaking them to a higher level of consciousness. The reader can decide for himself or herself how successful this particular experiment of Bharati's is in English.

2. Bharati's use of rhymes is both evocative and playful. His habit was clearly to think in poetry! A small point: the reader may also notice the use of special sonic patterns, like the similarity of the final consonants in 'faith' and 'death.' Tamil literature has a sophisticated understanding of similar sounds, including the recognition of various types of relationships based on specific syllables, consonants, and so on. An awareness of these interrelationships was second nature to Bharati.

3. In summary: 'A *Sada-Nishta,* who follows the Vedic sayings, does not think that there is such a thing as death in the world.'

4. A mystic who has realized God (definition from Bharati Prachuralayam).
5. Worlds.
6. Vehicle, embodiment (Bharati Prachuralayam).
7. As used by Bharati here, mind. This word is a term of profound significance in Indian philosophy; the work as a whole reflects the depth of Bharati's philosophical studies and his preoccupation with the kinds of mental and spiritual development that are emphasized in these traditions. At the very least, the influence of as Patanjali's *Yoga Sutra* is obvious.
8. Sport (Bharati Prachuralayam).
9. The ten incarnations of Vishnu; each had a specific purpose, to help humankind and destroy evil. See also note to Chapter 40, Love-Mad, above.
10. Soul; also *atman*. In Indian philosophy, the soul is considered to be devoid of attributes and indestructible, qualities that Bharati discusses further along in these 'Thoughts'.
11. The qualities: *sattva* (peaceful and quiet), *rajas* (aggressive), and *tamas* (slow and dull).
12. Free from the three gunas or attributes of matter (Bharati Prachuralayam).
13. A celestial tree that gives whatever is desired (Bharati Prachuralayam).

Index of Titles in Chronological Order

Index of Titles by
Original Journal Appearance

Arya
English Monthly edited by Sri Aurobindo, 1914-21

1. Andal, the Vaishnava Poetess
    May, 1915

2. To the Cuckoo

3. I Dreamed a Dream

4. Ye Others!

5. Nammalwar, the Supreme Vaishnava Saint and Poet
    July, 1915

6. Love-Mad
    July, 1915